CLIMB INTO THE THE BELL TOWER

Essays on Poetry

Myra Cohn Livingston

CLIMB INTO THE THE BELL TOWER

Essays on Poetry

HARPER & ROW, PUBLISHERS, New York

Grand Rapids, Philadelphia, St. Louis, San Francisco
London, Singapore, Sydney, Tokyo, Toronto

Climb Into the Bell Tower: Essays on Poetry
Copyright © 1990 by Myra Cohn Livingston
All rights reserved. No part of this book may be used or reproduced
in any manner whatsoever without written permission except in the
case of brief quotations embodied in critical articles and reviews.
Printed in the United States of America. For information address
Harper & Row Junior Books, 10 East 53rd Street, New York, NY 10022.
Typography by Al Cetta
1 2 3 4 5 6 7 8 9 10
First Edition

Library of Congress Cataloging-in-Publication Data
Livingston, Myra Cohn.
  Climb into the bell tower : essays on poetry / Myra Cohn
Livingston.
      p.   cm.
  ISBN 0-06-024015-6 : $. — ISBN 0-06-446100-9 (pbk.) :
$
  1. Children's poetry—History and criticism. I. Title.
PN1085.L59 1990   89-36412
809.1—dc20   CIP

In memory of
Richard Roland Livingston
1922-1990

Contents

Preface

The pilgrimage is not one of place. It has been many years since Horace Gregory sat in his closet office at Sarah Lawrence College; years since he leaned forward to emphasize a point about the "jackdaws" of poetry, and then—unexpectedly—rocked back with laughter, enjoying jokes that I have come to suspect were private, incomprehensible to a college student oblivious of the warfare engulfing academicians and the new schools of poetry raging even more fiercely today.

The pilgrimage is one of spirit, and if that spirit allows no rest, no steady rhythm, no resolution of form or content, it is because in that closet the whorls of smoke from his endless cigarettes, the unrestrained laughter, the whispered admonitions live a life of their own and ceaselessly haunt my work. "The trouble with you," he told me over and over again, "is that there are no devils in your world."

I know now that he was conjuring up these devils, breathing them out with each puff of smoke, seeking them out in books, pushing me to battle with them during a full year of writing heroic couplets. *The Duchess of Malfi*, the Staten Island ferry, the crazed woman on the subway—every observation and sound was subject to the discovery and restraints of that same classic form. Once, only once, did he allow an imitation of Praed and then only with a warning about the innocuous bed on which Helen Bevington had fainted.

The admonitions, the laughter within that closet, are not silenced. Once I had acknowledged those devils to which he had led me, they were sustained by a correspondence that illumines what he himself called the role of the responsible critic. Such a critic must cast aside fear, not be intimidated by the past, and encourage rediscoveries in reading. "Hawthorne in his note books," he wrote to me, "has a remarkable and vivid portrait of Tennyson shuffling down an art gallery. Look it up in Hawthorne's English note books." My enthusiasm for Edward Lear brought word from him that it was Eliot who rekindled interest in Lear in the twentieth century, who "appreciated fully the deeper and 'serious' undertones of Lear's nonsense. . . ."

"I have many things to talk to you about," another letter began, three pages in which he chided me for a title I had chosen for one of my books, a title that made him think of "finger painting" and made his "flesh creep." Yet there was praise for trying to raise standards in my own field, thanks for an article that established the importance of *The Crystal Cabinet* and *The Silver Swan*, for research that is, "I know, personal and painstaking, which makes both enemies and friends and requires courage, more courage than most people think in these bad times."

Often he would apologize for delays in correspondence. "I've just survived a terrific battle with myself," he wrote after a summer heat wave, or "I'm trying to give up cigarettes in toto. . . . Trying to cure a foolish bad habit is an unheroic task but one that should be done without too much self-pity. After all, I'm not mice but men."

A curious phrase that—not in the singular, but plural. And yet, armed with his shield of Achilles, his source of self-knowledge, his defense against the fatal wound, he understood the battles of flesh and mind. During a time when I sent him packages of sweets and tea, I began to understand his fascination with the cunning art that decorated his shield, and that kept him mindful of courage. "The tea, then," he wrote, "is all the more appreciated; of all vices it creates the mildest illusions, and an instant hallucination of general brightness. This last is something that coffee fails to do, for coffee merely forces us to think we are awake and fit to face the world. Most of us are kept alive and moving by our self-deceptions—which are so alluring that we out-face defeats and out-leap pitfalls. . . ."

The last time I saw Horace Gregory I was possessed with Ben Jonson. He wanted me to see and read from the heavy, worn leather volume of the "Masques" high on a shelf and asked his wife, Marya Zaturenska, to find it. It was an act of affection, a display for both of physical and emotional courage.

When the suppressed "Wasp in a Wig" chapter of *Alice* was published some years ago, I found myself again returning to his essay in *The Shield of Achilles* "Immortality and the White Knight of Lewis Carroll's *Alice*." It is a work

with layered meaning far beyond the immediate concerns of Wordsworth's "Ode" or the story of the Dormouse
with its "memory and muchness." We were both bothered
by an interruption in Alice's growth, and saw the need for
some explanation of this. A piece had long been missing.
He had sensed it intuitively; the Wasp episode pointed the
way to an answer. We had bouts of correspondence concerning Byron, Moore, Southey, Tennyson, and Wordsworth. He would attack and I would counter.

Several years ago a clue in George Steiner's *Tolstoy or
Dostoyevsky* led me back, once again, to the Gregory essay.
The illumination of the darkened path shone brightly:
"[Alice] knew terror, but not grief." But it was too late to
test the epiphany against the whisperings and the laughter.

Still and all, Horace Gregory had chosen Wordsworth
to begin his essay, words from "Intimations of Immortality."

> What though the radiance which was once so bright
> Be now for ever taken from my sight,
>   Though nothing can bring back the hour
> Of splendour in the grass, of glory in the flower;
>   We will grieve not, rather find
>   Strength in what remains behind;
>   In the primal sympathy
>   Which having been must ever be; . . .

Of late I have been rereading Ralph Waldo Emerson. It
is his essay on Montaigne that captures my attention, for
Emerson defines "skepticism" as "the attitude assumed by
the student in relation to particulars which society adores,
but which he sees to be reverend only in their tendency

and spirit." Society does indeed cling to its existing order, and "the interrogation of custom at all points is an inevitable stage" in the growth of the mind. This mind is often "equally at odds with the evils of society and with the projects that are offered to relieve them." While the skeptic knows that life is not so easy as schools and other institutions would have us believe, that one must take into account the "benevolences" of such establishments, still and all "there are doubts." And to know that one does not know is valuable.

How I should like to speak to Horace Gregory about this, yet now there can be no pilgrimage of place. Gregory, the poet, man, and teacher, is gone. All that remains are the devils, the spirit, and the shield.

—M C L
1990

CHOOSING
AND SHARING
POETRY

The Poem on Page 81

Pulling apart a poem is an act, I have usually found, better reserved for private moments, or those spent with older children seeking the means to answers in a creative-writing group. Nevertheless, in this act of experiencing one poem—in asking, as does John Ciardi, "how does a poem mean?"—are implicit a number of rather important matters.

The poem is Robert Frost's "The Pasture."

> I'm going out to clean the pasture spring;
> I'll only stop to rake the leaves away
> (And wait to watch the water clear, I may):
> I sha'n't be gone long.—You come too.
>
> I'm going out to fetch the little calf
> That's standing by the mother. It's so young
> It totters when she licks it with her tongue.
> I sha'n't be gone long.—You come too.

A first look at this poem (just as we might see a painting) shows us a boy (illustrators are inclined to dress him in overalls with a rake over his shoulder) going off to perform a few chores. He tells us that he must clean the pasture spring and fetch a calf.

But almost in the same second our auditory sense be-

3

comes involved (music might certainly play a part here), for we hear him talking to someone. Not only is he relating what he is going to do, but he is mentioning to an invisible someone that he "sha'n't be gone long.—You come too." He is extending an invitation, therefore, to join him.

Sharpening our vision and our hearing further, we become aware that the boy is more deeply involved than in simply doing two chores. For in the first stanza he tells the unseen someone that he *may wait* to watch the water clear—in other words, it is not mandatory he do so as part of his job; he does not *have* to do so; he *may*. In the second stanza the chore is simply to fetch the calf; that is all that is expected of him. But he tells us more: it is a little calf, a young calf standing by its mother; it totters when she licks it with her tongue.

We hear, therefore, if we listen, that the boy is not merely concerned with responsibilities and work, but that he is seeking something more: watching the water clear, watching the calf and its mother—acts of wonder and interest. These are the extras—the joys, the emotional involvement—far beyond duty.

Remember too that he is issuing an invitation to another; not to join and help with the work, but to share with him what follows. Perhaps he is not only seeking companionship, so as not to go it alone, but holding out to another a promise of something exciting and wonderful.

The invitation, you will note, is earnestly meant—for it is repeated in both stanzas of the poem, and is prefaced with man's eternal plea when he asks another to join him: It won't take much time. The gentle persuasion is there, repeated twice. Join me while I clean the pasture spring and rake the leaves away; perhaps I'll even stay on to watch the water clear. Join me while I fetch the calf; you'll have a chance to see how young it is, how little, how its mother licks it with her tongue, how it totters. This piece of description serves a twofold purpose, for it not only holds out the promise of seeing something special, but adds appeal to the invitation.

But now the poem becomes something more. It is no longer simply a boy on his chores; it beckons as the poet's invitation to all of us (you, me, the unseen invisible some-ones and everyones) to fulfill our chores and responsibilities, but to take a few moments to experience the serendipity of it all! To watch, to perceive, to marvel, to enjoy and observe matters as well as tend them. And the twice-repeated invitation—"You come too." We must, in our lives, do our work as expected, but must we not also take a few moments to pause and reflect, to enjoy the wonders about us, to become emotionally involved?

Is Robert Frost speaking of a boy going out to do his chores, or is he saying much, much more?

Here is another of Frost's poems, "Stopping by Woods on a Snowy Evening."

Whose woods these are I think I know.
His house is in the village though;
He will not see me stopping here
To watch his woods fill up with snow.

My little horse must think it queer
To stop without a farmhouse near
Between the woods and frozen lake
The darkest evening of the year.

He gives his harness bells a shake
To ask if there is some mistake.

The only other sound's the sweep
Of easy wind and downy flake.

The woods are lovely, dark and deep,
But I have promises to keep,
And miles to go before I sleep,
And miles to go before I sleep.

In this poem Frost speaks of the same thing, but at another
stage in life; here we see not a boy but a man, who, in
the midst of "promises" and "miles to go," has stopped to
watch the beauty of the woods filling up with snow. His
horse, understandably, must think him queer; an animal
is not capable of comprehending why a man needs to pause
and observe this side of life, far from even a farmhouse on the darkest evening of the year; nor would the
owner of the woods, whose house is comfortably in the
village. "He will not see me stopping here," the man tells
us; there is no chance of his being seen and possibly ridiculed by another human being. Yet, realizing all this, he
must stop to satisfy his desire for beauty—in spite of "promises to keep" and "miles to go before I sleep . . . and
miles to go before I sleep."

A child would respond differently to this second poem;
perhaps not respond at all, for it views man at a stage not
fathomed by childhood. The known chores of the boy are
not those of the man; his promises are shrouded in mystery
and he is much nearer to "sleep" (with all of its implications)
than a boy. Nor would a child hesitate to issue an invitation
to another to join and marvel with him. A man, alas, knows
better than to ask another to share with him a display of
emotion.

But both poems, outpourings of what Yevtushenko has

called Robert Frost's "healthy peasant wisdom," are master-pieces of understatement and, though geared to different age levels—one through a repeated invitation from a boy, and one through an implicit understanding of how queer such an invitation would seem—speak to us of the same thing. Speak to us of our emotions, our experience, in a way only poetry can! Could there be a more meaningful invitation for us or for the children we know?

It is most interesting that in an article titled "Where Are We Going with Poetry for Children?" Patrick J. Groff, a professor of education at San Diego State College, defines very neatly something no one else I have ever read has been able to do—what poetry for children is. The very term "Poetry for Children" seems moot, for I have come to think in terms of poetry children enjoy, or poetry to which children respond. In any case, Groff rejects any definition based on an emotional approach and chides Eleanor Farjeon for not being able to define poetry, remarking that her question in the poem "What Is Poetry? Who Knows?" expresses false bewilderment. Groff writes:

> The definition is apprehensible and to the point: poetry for children is writing that (in addition to using, in most cases, the mechanics of poetry) transcends the literal meaning of expository writing. . . . It is writing that goes beyond the immediately obvious . . . [it] consists of those aspects of writing that cannot be readily explained, unless one has some knowledge of what is going on. In contrast to that which is readily and completely understandable to all, poetry is often ambiguous.

One may or may not agree with this definition. The point is that, even should it be acceptable, what follows in the article is a source of amazement to me. For the writer now speaks of Frost's "The Pasture." I quote:

> "The Pasture" tested against this definition is revealed as a poem only in the mechanical sense. True, it has some poetic features: a certain cadence, rhyme, and some slight inversion of sentence pattern—"And wait to watch the water clear, I may." (The word order seems used largely to satisfy a rhyme scheme, "away-may.") The poem does have a refrain, and even a colloquial word, "sha'n't" (if colloquialisms are poetic). But these are all a part of the mechanics of poetry. To identify a poem on the basis of such elements is too easy. . . . Obviously to define poetry merely in terms of its mechanical features does not take much perception or maturity.

The article continues:

> In another sense, "The Pasture" is not exceptional poetry because with startlingly few changes the poem could be made into a paragraph of prose. To show this, drop the first refrain in the poem and put the third line into a regular pattern.

(What he says here, of course, is that the first invitation might just as well be omitted!)

And later on, his concluding remarks about the poem are: ". . . in 'The Pasture' the emphasis on subject denies the poem much status as poetry."

Now, I would not be nearly so concerned with Groff's indictment of "The Pasture" if I felt that he was a stupid man, an uninformed man, a man unaware of what goes into the making of a poem, instead of a man whose opinions I have read and enjoyed in the past. But he has obviously given poetry much thought, for earlier in the article he pointedly rejects one definition of a poem as "merely a reconstruction of an experience." With this I agree. He has, moreover, very clearly stated his understanding of the fact that words in poetry have more meaning than they do in prose. I quote again.

> Words possess suggested significances apart from their explicit and recognized meanings. It is the guessing element that requires the reader to go below the surface of words, to plumb their literal meanings. Figurative language most often provides the guessing element. A poem without metaphor, simile, hyperbole, personification, metonymy must compensate for the loss of these poetic devices in some other way. Sometimes it is in the use of words of a certain tone, for in poetry, the language, not the subject, is of utmost importance.

In other words, Groff understands intellectually very well the use of words and language, the tone. He recognizes that a poet must use a certain means to express his meaning. Yet he utterly fails to look beyond the technical features of "The Pasture"; indeed, he has separated the "means" from the meaning. In poetry this cannot be done. Both are inexorably entwined; part of each other.

He does not seem to realize, for example, that there is more to Frost's use of "I may" and "away" than a rhyme scheme. The "I may," coming where it does at the end of a line, occurs as the sort of offhand remark a boy would make. Frost has, in fact, put parentheses around the entire line to emphasize the point. I might even venture the guess that Frost, in writing this poem, made "I may" the focal point and chose "away" to complete the rhyme scheme.

So what Groff refers to, casually, as an inverted sentence pattern seems to me to be almost at the crux of what the poem is saying.

Enough of technicalities; what I am interested in pointing out is that the writer seems not to allow himself to experience poetry, to feel it, to (in his own words) "plumb" the words. He is so obsessed with technicalities and definitions that he fails to allow himself to respond or react. He may look, but he does not see. He may listen, but he does not hear. Somewhat earlier in the article he has even dismissed among many others a claim that poetry allows children to experience life in a deeper sense. It may happen, he admits, if a poem and a child hit it off, but prose does this just as well, if not better. To Groff, therefore, poetry, may be embarrassing when one has to involve his emotions. Poetry in his terms, at least to me, can never be a meaningful experience.

Now this is not to say that I view "The Pasture" as the masterpiece of all poetry, nor that I ask him or you to find in it the ultimate. But when he says that "What is poetry for one person is not poetry for another" is an illogical statement, I must counter that to me it is a most logical statement, for it admits that each of us is constructed in a different and unique way, and the poem that sings or speaks through words and music to one of us may not touch another.

But to define everything on a logical basis, channel all things through the intellect, block off emotions when they do not fit within a pat definition, and categorize what lies outside of this definition as without "much status" strikes me as an apology for emotions, a feeling of embarrassment about them. It is a source of wonder to me.

Why does it happen? Perhaps it is the curse of our scientific age; that we are so beset by labels and definitions, so busy fitting things into compartments, dealing with facts and figures, cataloging and computing, that we fail to feel the meanings behind the things. I think, perhaps, that a good part of the answer lies in our strangled emotions; "strangled" is perhaps a strong word, yet it seems apt. Does this spring from our Calvinistic, Puritanical tradition, which we seem in the process of losing, but which is still very much with most of us? Has it been buried in the root of our culture too long? Do we shrink from emotion, afraid that we will be thought immature—weak should we cry, foolish if we laugh? Many emotions are diverted by reading, many released in a darkened theater, through motion pictures or television, many on the football or baseball field, in the grandstands, many at the fights.

The crime of our civilization, Archibald MacLeish has said, is that we do not feel: "To feel emotion is at least to feel. . . . If poetry can call our numbed emotions to life, its plain human usefulness needs no further demonstration." How beautifully he points out that while the mind alone cannot logically make sense out of images (the stuff of poetry), emotion can, feeling can. Is there any better example than Patrick Groff defining poetry neatly, understanding all of the materials with which a poet shapes his poem, yet failing to *feel* what a poet is saying?

The intellect tells us, reason tells us, of course, that there is a time and a place to smother emotions. Many adults stood aghast at the arrival of *Harriet the Spy*, *Dorp Dead*, *Durango Street*. Is it necessary, they asked, that children should know of violence, of spying, of plotted murder, of cruelty, of the baser emotions? A few even doubted that young children should see the place where the wild things are—fear, terror, death, nontruths. But what can we know of peace, truth, the Ten Commandments, if we know not their opposites?

Those who would attempt to smother the ogres of fairy tales, water down the witches, have risen again and again only to be quelled, for, as Lewis Mumford so aptly commented in speaking of the anti-fantasy pro-here-and-now movement, "We did not get rid of the dragon; we only banished St. George." Television commercials with their varying monsters, doves that fly in the window to magically soothe dishpan hands, translucent cages that conveniently fly stuffy sinuses to Arizona—these will always be with us in one form or another because they fulfill a need. What we all seek, of course, is a more meaningful sort of fantasy, one that does not only embody escape, but enriches. How unbelievably encouraging it is that Frodo, Bilbo, and J. R. R. Tolkien have been welcomed by people of all ages, including our thinking young college students.

For Sartre, even Jean Paul Sartre, recognized the value of his early boyhood escape reading: "The return to order was always accompanied by progress: the heroes were rewarded; they received honors, tokens of admiration, money; thanks to their dauntlessness, a territory had been conquered, a work of art had been protected. . . . From these books I derived my most deep-seated phantasmagoria: optimism."

Optimism! I am optimistic. I feel that when emotions come out into the open, whether in the form of what seems to me rather peculiar, but certainly emotional, dancing such as our teenagers do; when marches and even strikes and riots break a heretofore passive populace (although I would prefer protest to be in another form); when the mode of dress changes (although I myself prefer a neater and more kempt look)—when emotions come out into the open, it is a healthy sign. What is more fearful is that they be strangled and smothered. "To feel emotion is at least to feel."

When we do not question the neat definition, when we fail to feel and experience the meaning behind the words, relating it to our own emotions, then, and only then, are we lost.

And what has all this to do with the poetry we share with children?

Poetry, however else it may be defined, carries with it appeal to the emotions . . . "a more than usual state of emotion," in the words of Samuel Coleridge; what Louise Bogan and William Jay Smith in their introduction to *The Golden Journey* call "many kinds of emotion which prose cannot convey." Whether it be the gay, singsong, simple rhymes of Mother Goose that amuse the very young; or the recognition of the world about him that a young child will find captured by rhyme and music, a certain reinforcement of experience, most easily communicated and understood in brief word form; or whether it touch the older child by its insistence upon, as Wallace Stevens has written, "a tune beyond us, yet ourselves"—still, it must touch the emotions. It would seem to follow, therefore, that when we are thinking of poetry to share with children, we take into account the subject, but far more pertinent, those emotions that are within the range of childhood. Since all poetry is made of words caught up in a pattern of music, it is doubtful that we need dwell on the mechanics, the feet, the rhyme or nonrhyme (note the popularity of haiku).

We need rather to probe what lies behind what the poet is saying. Does it relate to the emotions and experiences of the younger ages? Do we need to stick to the poets of childhood, or should we rather choose from all poetry with an eye and ear to what a poet is saying in a particular poem that might have meaning, value, and enrichment through an essential enjoyment for children, or a particular child?

There is, of course, no easy guide, no formula for finding such poems. They are met in anthologies, in collections, in magazines, in odd and assorted places. What one does learn is that surprise is at every turn—a poem that appeals to one seven-year-old will pass his neighbor by; subjects that delight girls may bore boys and vice versa. Words that set one child to laughing will leave others in silence. One learns, too, that it is not always at the nursery-school level that Mother Goose is best received. Level of achievement, socioeconomic factors play a big part in the sort of response a poem may meet.

Nor will the poems one generation enjoys necessarily be meaningful to the next. It struck me as interesting, during a recent rereading of Vachel Lindsay's *The Congo and Other Poems*, published in 1914, that I have seen and heard dozens of times his "Explanation of the Grasshopper":

> The Grasshopper, the grasshopper,
> I will explain to you:—
> He is the Brownies' racehorse,
> The fairies' Kangaroo.

Brownies today are better known as little Girl Scouts, and fairies go in and out of vogue. Perhaps, then, it would be wise to use instead an earlier poem called "The Lion":

The Lion is a kingly beast
He likes the Hindu for a feast.
And if no Hindu he can get,
The lion family is upset.

He cuffs his wife and bites her ears
Till she is nearly moved to tears.
Then some explorer finds the den
And all is family peace again.

Not a great poem, but certainly more in tune with our times!

"The Blue Fairy!" a nine-year-old boy snorted at me one day at the museum. I was telling him about Pinocchio. "There's no such thing as a fairy!" In his world all that mattered was outer space and Martian men. The fact that the Blue Fairy and men from Mars might have something in common rather intrigued him. I took him a copy of the poem "Go Fly a Saucer" by David McCord.

I've seen one flying saucer. Only when
It flew across our sight in 1910
We little thought about the little men.

But let's suppose the little men were there
To cozy such a disc through foreign air:
Connecticut was dark, but didn't scare.

I wonder what they thought of us, and why
They chose the lesser part of Halley's sky,
And went away and let the years go by

Without return? Or did they not get back
To Mars or Venus through the cosmic flak?
At least they've vanished, every spaceman Jack.

> Now they are with us in the books, in air,
> In argument, in hope, in fear, in spare
> Reports from men aloft who saw them there.
>
> The day one saucer cracks, the greatest egg
> Since dinosaur and dodo shook a leg
> Will give new meaning to the prefix *meg.*
>
> Some say the saucers with their little race
> Of little men from Littlesphere in space
> Have sensed our international disgrace.
>
> And when the thing blows over, up, or what,
> They'll gladly land and give us all they've got
> So Earth shall cease to be a trouble spot.
>
> One fact is old as Chaucer, Saucer Men:
> You may be little as a bantam hen,
> But Earth has specialized in little men.

Now here were creatures of fantasy that were believable! And to express his delight, the nine-year-old began to write poems for me.

Pink, sugary-smiling fairies dressed in gossamer are, for the most part, vanishing. In their stead are creatures of the imagination with more blood, bone, and downright character. No longer passive and goody-goody, they display astoundingly realistic emotions!

The dwarfs in *The Hobbit*:

> Chip the glasses and crack the plates!
>   Blunt the knives and bend the forks!
> That's what Bilbo Baggins hates—
>   Smash the bottles and burn the corks!

The Stone Troll who steals a shinbone from the grave of Tom Bombadil's uncle and gives Tom a good kick when he asks that it be returned:

> Troll sat alone on his seat of stone,
> And munched and mumbled a bare old bone;
> For many a year he had gnawed it near,
> For meat was hard to come by.
> Done by! Gum by!
> In a cave in the hills he dwelt alone,
> And meat was hard to come by. . . .

A far cry, indeed, from Rose Fyleman:

> Have you watched the fairies when the rain is done,
> Spreading out their little wings to dry them in the sun.
> I have! I have! Isn't it fun?

Harry Behn is in tune with "The Gnome":

> I saw a gnome
> As plain as plain
> Sitting on top
> Of a weathervane.
>
> He was dressed like a crow
> In silky black feathers
> And there he set watching
> All kinds of weathers.
>
> He talked like a crow too,
> Caw caw caw,
> When he told me exactly
> What he saw,
>
> Snow to the north of him
> Sun to the south,

And he spoke with a beaky
Kind of a mouth.

But he wasn't a crow,
That was plain and plain
'Cause crows never sit
On a weathervane.

What I saw was simply
A usual gnome
Looking things over
On his way home.

Children are not to be deceived. The subject matter we
share with them may delight, but try to place it in a false
landscape, in false emotions, and they will, as Paul Hazard
tells us, rightfully reject it. Why else have we lost the didactic
turn-of-the-century verse?

Oh Mary this will never do.
Your work is sadly done, I fear.
And such a little of it, too;
You have not taken pains, my dear. . . .

Children not only shun didactic and moral verse (that
so-called poetry in which the writer sermonizes directly)
but almost insist on what Marianne Moore has called in
poetry "imaginary gardens with real toads." Children love
imaginary gardens, even as we ourselves do, but they insist
the toads be real!

Even in Edward Lear, where there is undisguised fun in
an imaginary world, silly things happen, but they happen
in spite of and because of very human emotions. The table
complains to the chair of chilblains on her feet; the kangaroo
cautions the duck to sit quite steady on the way to the

Dee and Jelly-Bo-Lee; the owl charms the pussycat with words of romantic endearment; the Jumblies reject the plea of those who fear they will drown in their sieve. And who but children (or the children in us) would but doubt that a woman's chin might grow sharp enough to use for playing a harp, or that a man's beard might well house owls, wren, larks, and a hen.

Even in the most realistic of poems, the realm of the imagination has play in the poet's world, his garden as it were. But it must be peopled with those who bear some resemblance to what the child knows is genuine, deeply and honestly felt.

And this, I think, is precisely where the difficulty lies in our attempts to work with poetry. For so often we feel a gross inadequacy in ourselves; we feel shy, embarrassed, afraid. And this is the result of not living fully enough in the poet's garden, of not letting our emotions, just for a little time, rule our heads!

Poets, after all, are human beings. They just happen to be sensitive to their world; they have something to say about their experiences in and relationships to this world, so strongly that they must share it with others in the hope that others, too, will feel what they are saying as it applies to their experiences and relationships. And they capture it in what they believe to be the most suitable and appealing means—words, the eternal and intuitive sense of and need for rhythm, music.

What distinguishes the poem from mere verse or rhyme (for the form seems similar enough) are the voices of the poets; their courage, if you will, to seize hold of the experience, the object, and turn it into meaningful shape. This, of course, demands that poets deeply involve themselves, laying their emotions bare. To search out poetry, therefore, we must listen to the poets, hear what they are saying. If we shy away from this, we end up with only a meaningless analysis, a ripping apart of words and feet, and except for some extraneous rhymes something just as well said in prose.

For poets need readers, just as they need the world around them. Frost has talked of the "right reader."

I am not suggesting that many of us have the time to pull apart poems and view them in perspective. But I do believe that we should allow ourselves the time to stop, occasionally, and become "right readers," not through analysis of metrics and inverted sentences, not through rhyme, but in the giving of our feelings and sensitivities to what lies behind the words.

A piece of advice I have often heard given is to only read a poem that one, oneself, likes. The enthusiasm of the reader is carried over to others. I think this is good counsel, but I would hope that those who share poetry would go one step further, not just digging into a neat little storehouse, but searching out more poems, new poems. It is a commitment, but a rewarding one.

Giving back poetry to children as an emotional experience often means stepping on toes. The "purposeful" method of the classroom, where poems are given as exercises in finding verbs, descriptive words, rhyming words, capital letters, must inevitably be encountered and quashed. It is important to me, before reading poetry with a group, to explain that no person in the group will like, or be expected to like, all of the poems. To admit that each of us has a different makeup, with varying sensitivities and reactions, takes the onus out of that elusive "beauty" with which poetry supposedly abounds.

How much more realistic, how much more honest, to allow a child room for emotions, room to respond to that poem or that within the poem that touches that child.

Here is a poem I found on page 81 of the anthology *Up the Line to Death*:

Up and down, up and down
They go, the gray rat, and the brown.
The telegraph lines are tangled hair,
Motionless on the sullen air;
An engine has fallen on its back,
With crazy wheels, on a twisted track;
All ground to dust is the little town;
Up and down, up and down
They go, the gray rat, and the brown.
A skull, torn out of the graves nearby,
Gapes in the grass. A butterfly,
In azure iridescence new,
Floats into the world, across the dew;
Between the flow'rs. Have we lost our way,
Or are we toys of a god at play,
Who do these things on a young Spring day?

Where the salvo fell, on a splintered ledge
Of ruin, at the crater's edge,
A poppy lives: and young, and fair,
The dewdrops hang on the spider's stair,
With every rainbow still unhurt
From leaflet unto leaflet girt.
Man's house is crushed; the spider lives:
Inscrutably He takes, and gives,

Who guards not any temple here,
Save the temple of the gossamer.

Up and down, up and down
They go, the gray rat, and the brown:
A pistol cracks: they too are dead.

The nightwind rustles overhead.

This poem "After the Salvo" by Herbert Asquith, is unique for its widely varying imagery, even apart from its sobering meaning. You will hear it differently, feel it differently from the nine-, ten-, and eleven-year-olds whose expression and emotional responses go into clay, ink, collage, and paint at the Los Angeles County Museum of Art.

This was their response: One girl pictured the rats as symbols of evil, each with its shadow. To another the rats were only toy mice, climbing up a hickory-dickory clock. A boy turned the engine upright and drew it with mechanical precision; several other children depicted it upside down on twisted track. A skull emerged in one picture. A graveyard with tombstones dominated another. A huge black spider was drawn over and over again, on three pieces of paper, by a seemingly placid nine-year-old girl who later confided that a horror–science fiction film depicting giant spiders that she had seen on television at the age of four had bothered her ever since. Hitler dominated one picture. Another girl splattered paint at random on a piece of paper and labeled it "Destruction." Someone took wood and wire to make a sculpture of the twisted track. One boy put into a glorious pastel drawing all of the images plus buildings and trappings of a town. Butterflies were flying across one paper. Flowers were the subject of another. All but butterflies, flowers, and grass were done in deep reds, browns, black, and gold paint.

Unlike many other class sessions during which poems were read, in this one not one child failed to respond.

What definition is there to encompass all the poems that have meaning and appeal to children? Do not definitions belong, rather, to science, to the laboratory? Our varying emotions, our needs as human beings, are not so easily stuffed into formulas and test tubes. The language of experience, of feeling, is not, as Ciardi so well points out, the language of classification, and the point of poetry is not to arrive at a definition but to arrive at an experience—to feel, to bring our emotions and sensitivities into play.

In a poem, says MacLeish, the poet gives us a "means to meaning"—the meaning of our human experience. If we refuse to involve ourselves in more than its technical appearance, if we ask "What does it mean?" rather than "How does it mean?" we have only cheated ourselves.

You may remember the Philosopher in James Stephens's *The Crock of Gold*; the philosopher who lived only by reason, fact, and intellect until his interview with Angus Ogg. "He had stamped up the hill with vigour" for the encounter. "He strode down it in ecstacy." "I have learned," said the Philosopher, "that the head does not hear anything until the heart has listened, and that what the heart knows today, the head will understand tomorrow."

I believe that science occupies an important place in our world, as does its very basis of being, fact. I believe that responsibility and work are important, but so, also, is the pause for reflection, for searching into the meanings of our experiences. I believe in the power of emotions, the creativity they unleash into and through art, music, dance, and poetry. And I believe in discovering imaginary gardens with real toads; in searching for the means with which to bring delight and enjoyment back into poetry; in extending an invitation to children through poetry to not merely look and listen, but see—and hear.

You come too.

Beginnings

All things are weak and tender at birth. Therefore we must have our eyes open to the beginnings; for as then, when a thing is little, we do not discover its danger, so when it is grown we no longer discover the remedy for it.

—Michel de Montaigne

How well we, as teachers, know the truth of these words written over four hundred years ago! They are part of our daily experience watching, as we do, elementary-school children in their formative years approach their peers, their relationships, their studies, their trust and faith in us in the classroom. Experience has helped us spot the shy, the troublemaker, the emotionally disturbed, the achiever, the child who is burdened with some fleeting, perhaps, but very real problem. It is our job and profession to do this— or why else would we be teachers? We know we must "have our eyes open" with our beginning children, for if we overlook the danger signs that call for us to aid and help, nurture and foster any individual, we not only fail to discharge our responsibilities but we send on to upper levels, to high school and college and life, young people ill equipped to fulfill their potential for themselves or for society.

It is indeed being made very clear to us, in all levels of life today, that we need many remedies for the college student who cannot write a composition, or for those young people who have not the aptitude for college and cannot even fill out a job application. Our task, therefore, as elementary teachers is monumental. It is not an easy responsibility, and in order to "have our eyes open" we must often summon experts in the field, psychologists, eminent educators, and textbook writers who help us to teach skills. Not one of us, to paraphrase John Donne, is capable of being an island.

And yet, how very peculiar that we understand this, that we struggle with the nonreader, the troublemaker, the disturbed—that we are willing to work and build and help, sometimes to tear ourselves apart, to guide "the weak and tender," that we recognize it is not easy to fill a young mind and heart with all the information and skills and richness it needs, and yet, when it comes to the arts, that great body of aesthetic experience that enriches an individual's life for as long as life is given, we seek the easy way out. We have become willing to accept anything the child produces as art, guised in those enigmatic phrases "artistic expression" and "creativity," and we have allowed our children to believe that they are "young authors" and "poets." We have come to praise and publish their work in photocopied booklets, school newsletters, thick offset bound or stapled collections, as well as hardbound trade books and magazines. We have swallowed whole the idea that there is poetry in all children and that whatever they write should be accepted and, unfortunately far too often, held up as a model to other children.

Montaigne has written that "as when a thing is little, we do not discover its danger, so when it is grown we no longer discover the remedy for it."

The danger, alas, is very real to me. Are we, I wonder, being fair to the children? Do they not deserve more from us as teachers? If they are told that they are "poets" and "authors" in their very earliest years, is this not false praise? Do they not need to know that they are only just beginning—that the way toward true achievement is long and difficult? Why is it that we insist that every child is a "poet"? Every child is not a good reader, apt in mathematics, or a cracker-jack baseball player; every child is not a dancer or talented in drawing. But somehow we have jumped on a bandwagon that, if continued, I fear will produce one of the most frustrated and despondent generations of all times; they will have been led to believe that they are Titans, that hard work, disappointment, and failure no longer matter in the world. It is one thing to speak of things being easy, when one no longer has to scrub clothes by a riverbank, to journey by wagon train, to chop wood for heat, to travel miles by foot to borrow a book; that is a type of ease that enables human beings to expend their energies on other pursuits. But let us not confuse this kind of hard work with the soul-searching, perseverance, difficulty, and sweat that the production of a true artifact requires of the artist.

"Education," says John Ciardi, "is not possible without failure." "Arts," I heard Isaac Stern say on National Public

Radio, "can only exist when individuals are given the right to fail."

In a May Hill Arbuthnot Lecture, Molly Hunter concluded her speech (based on the idea that there must be a person behind the book, a paraphrase of Emerson) with these words:

> The child that was myself was born with a little talent, and I have worked hard, hard, hard, to shape it. Yet even this could not have made me a writer, for there is no book can tell anything worth saying unless life itself has first said it to the person who conceived that book. A philosophy *has* to be hammered out, a mind shaped, a spirit tempered. This is true for all of the craft. It is the basic process which must happen before literature can be created. It is also the final situation in which the artist is fully fledged; and because of the responsibilities involved, these truths apply most sharply to the writer who aspires to create literature for children.
>
> Especially for this writer, talent is not enough—no, by God, it is not! Hear this, critics, editors, publishers, parents, teachers, librarians—all of you who will shortly pick up a children's book to read it, or even glance idly through it. There *must* be a person behind that book.

Can we expect elementary-school children to have hammered out a philosophy, to have shaped minds and tempered spirits? Can they be, in yet a formative stage, *persons* in the sense of being able to create what is so offhandedly praised and called "poetry"?

It is odd for me to realize that for years I have been devoting myself to the process of helping children toward the writing of poetry. No one can teach creative writing, as I stated in my own book on the subject (*When You Are Alone/It Keeps You Capone: An Approach to Creative Writing with Children*). One can only make children aware of their sensitivities, and help children learn of the forms, the basic tools of poetry, into which they can put their own voices. During these years I have touched the lives of thousands of children and I have given praise when it is due and criticism when it is warranted. But I have never told children that they are *poets*, for I know only too well the years and work it takes to be considered a poet.

Yet we call our children "poets." Is it any wonder that a broadside from the Westwood Theatre announced a lecture series advertising Rod McKuen as "the world's most successful poet"? Aside from the sad fact that in our society "success" is equated with dollars rather than contribution or talent, I could not help but think: What sort of an education have we given our youth that Rod McKuen represents the ultimate in poetry? Is this the sort of poet we will continue to praise, to spawn and emulate? Somehow, in the words of Shakespeare and Hamlet, "the currents turn awry/And lose the name of action."

The tragedy of Hamlet, of course, is that his own action came too late. His many attempts to set things aright were but inept beginnings, and in the process lives were destroyed—in the end, his very own. I do not suggest that we will lose lives because of shortsightedness, but I do feel that unless we recognize the danger, it will soon be too late to "discover the remedy." Certainly we are all aware of a full-blown interest in poetry these days, which was not true even twenty years ago. To rethink what has happened during these past years may be of some value in considering how we might, as teachers, make some new beginnings.

When Harry Behn's *Cricket Songs* was published, Harry was ecstatic that teachers and children were interested in the book and that children were writing their own haiku. I voiced to him my concerns that the very difficult rules that govern haiku could be handled by most children, pointing out that, compressed as it is, haiku is perhaps the most difficult kind of poem to write well. Several years before his death we talked about this again. Harry, too, lamented that the haiku had lost all vestige of its original impact, that in the hands of the commercial market it had become an excuse for unscholarly slim volumes, that teachers had seized upon it as a break from rhyme and turned it into nothing more than a mathematical exercise of three lines with five, seven, and five syllables. It is most tempting to quote a few of the thousands of so-called haiku written by children that I have seen proudly displayed at school open houses or published in magazines and books, as well as examples of the bastardizing of Adelaide Crapsey's American variant on the haiku, a form called the cinquain, which, also nonrhyming, extended the three lines into five and allowed more freedom for thought in its two-, four-, six-, eight-, two-syllable pattern. Well-meaning, no doubt, but misguided educational firms and teachers invented their own variants, resulting in such things as "word cinquains" or "grammar poems" that only proved that a child could recognize nouns, adjectives, participles; write a sentence; and supply an antonym or synonym, according to the prescription. I daresay that a great deal of the teaching I now do is extremely touchy, for children will bring me their haiku and cinquains, written in English classes, that are so foreign to the spirit and form of the originals that, whereas I cannot in front of the child censure the teacher who has given the child an A, I must begin anew to teach what a haiku and cinquain really are! But what of the children who have been told that they are "poets" and that they have already achieved?

It takes hard work and time to write a poem, and the mistaken notion that writing poetry is "easy," that anyone can do it, continues, unfortunately, to flourish. The irreparable damage we have done to many children, throughout all of this, cannot be measured.

Concurrent with this misuse of form are several other schools of poetry writing with which I am sure you are familiar. On the one hand are teachers who believe that poetry must be about nature or happy-day events, who subscribe to what I call the "Truth, Beauty, and Wisdom" approach. These teachers fail to recognize that anything is a suitable subject for a poem and that rhyme is only one tool, not a necessity, for poetry. On the other hand we have the influence of the New York and Beat schools of poetry, to whom rhyme and meter are dirty words, who themselves write and encourage children to write down anything and call it a "poem."

Those of you who may know of my own poetry will recognize that I was trained in the school of rhyme/meter/form, that my first book, *Whispers and Other Poems*, written when I was eighteen, is clearly in this tradition, but that over the years I have experimented with free verse and that my books *The Malibu, The Way Things Are*, and *4-Way Stop* reflect a fluctuation between the more formal and freer expression. I feel there are strengths and weaknesses in both schools for myself and for the children I

teach. But when it comes to the fill-in school, I must admit
that I see a blazing red! For here is a lack of respect for
the intelligence of both teacher and child, an assumption
that neither is capable of having any creative spark, that
both must be spoon-fed with opening lines, mediocre cartoons, lists of words, the very lines on which to write, ad
nauseum. Although I admit that some teaching materials
are a shade better than others, the workbook that tells children they *are* poets or authors, asks them to respond to
pictures that may be of no particular interest, offers them
smell cards or prerecorded sounds, quite sickens me. I
have written at length of this in my books and articles and
I capsulize it now only as background for the dangers of
which Montaigne speaks.

Most fortunately, I am not alone in my observation of
the dangers. Writing of the background for *English Journal*'s
Poetry Festival, Nancy Larrick lamented that so many of
the poetry entries were about profound and philosophical
subjects, that the poems submitted contained poetically
stilted language, that there was an abuse of adjectives (if
not overuse), that much of the work was filled with cliché,
and that poor alignment was used in much of the free
verse. These are matters well worth pointing out, and although I would not go so far as to totally agree with her
idea of the "throwing over of rhyme," I do agree that when
we are trying to free the child from *meaningless* rhyme
"free verse . . . seems to invite creative thinking and often
provides the vehicle for truly poetic ideas and language."
We know, as teachers, that rhyme in the hands of a young
child can be a stifling and oftentimes ridiculous tool, but
my years of teaching have also proved to me that, when

carefully taught, children as early as second grade can learn to use it well. It is not easy—but it can be done. In the words of Jorge Luis Borges:

> You have to be far more skillful technically to attempt free verse than to attempt what you may think of as being old-fashioned. Of course, if you happen to be Walt Whitman, you'll have the inner strength, or inner urge, that makes you capable and worthy of free verse, but this doesn't happen to many of us . . . my advice to young people is to begin with the classical forms of verse and only after that become revolutionary. I remember an observation by Oscar Wilde— a prophetic observation. He said, "Were it not for the sonnet, the set forms of verse, we should all be at the mercy of genius." This is what's happening today; at least this is what's happening in my country. Almost every day I receive books of verse that put me at the mercy of genius—that is to say, books that seem to me quite meaningless. Even the metaphors in them are not discernible. Metaphor supposedly links two things, but in these books I see no links whatever. I get the impression that the whole thing has been done in a haphazard way, as though by a crazy computer of some kind. And I am expected to feel or enjoy something! . . . What I'm saying is that, in the long run, to break the rules, you must know *about* the rules.

To which I can only add Amen, and perhaps it is so with you. This is why I am at a loss to explain the popularity and blind acceptance of what followed in that issue of *English Journal* and in countless other institutional and commercial publications—gimmicks and ideas and suggestions that might possibly have some meaning for studying language arts, but most *certainly* contribute nothing to the writing of poetry. Among these are the suggestions to: (1) *Read the title of a poem and ask the students what the poem will be about; put the ideas on the board and revise or expand them as the poem's meaning unfolds.* Of what possible use can this be? Does the double meaning of Robert Frost's "The Pasture" make itself clear by the title? What about Emily Dickinson or e. e. cummings or Lewis Carroll, who chose to ignore titles? (2) *Encourage students to write lyrics to well-known tunes.* Is this not, I ask you, simply another variant on the fill-in school? (3) *Print lyrics to popular songs, distribute them and analyze the lyrics with the class. "Some questions students might want to explore are: What do the songs tell you about contemporary society? What is the subject matter of the poem? What metaphors does the author use to describe his feelings? Does the meter or rhythm of the poem enhance the sentiment?"* Why? If we are going to devote all this time to analyzing and pulling apart and finding metaphors and going into the very intricate study of meter and rhythm, why not choose recognized poets, Wallace Stevens or Langston Hughes or Richard Wilbur? Why settle for less than the best? (4) *"Read or ask the children to read the children's book* Happiness Is . . . Ask them to write their own metaphors for other words. The list might include: love, hate, school, nonsense, misery, liberation, war or intelligence."* Not only is this a language-arts exercise, but it is built on the premise that children are capable of metaphor—a difficult assignment for a full-fledged poet, let alone a young child. (5) *Write an acrostic poem.* Why? This is only proof that a child can write a name vertically and fill in words that begin with certain letters. (6) *Illustrate a narrative poem in comic-book style.* Why? Is this how we go about "Teaching Poetry"? (7) *Write* *a "Grammar Poem." Use one noun, two adjectives, three verbs, one phrase, and one synonym.* Here we are back to the misuse of the cinquain. And on and on and on.

What is the writing of poetry anyhow—a game? I recall articles in which teachers proudly proclaim that they "tricked" their students into writing poetry. I have seen the word "creativity" applied to solving puzzles, picking out sets of rhyming words, cutting words and piecing them together to make a so-called found poem (which only proves that the child can recognize a word and its relation to another word and perhaps construct a sentence). I have seen Poets-in-the-Schools make children believe they have created a poem by supplying them with a series of rubber stamps that contain words and have only to be pressed onto a stamp pad, and presto!—a poem. I have seen words put on cards, thrown into the middle of a room, and children asked to choose five or ten and make of these a "poem" with no regard to whether or not one word was meaningful to that child. Quite recently I saw an article on the limerick, which quite properly told that a limerick has five lines, that the first, second, and fifth rhyme and the third and fourth use a different rhyme, and that a limerick should be funny. But what did the author mean that lines one, two, and five have three beats and lines three and four have two beats? There was no mention that the beat, in this case, is what is called a metrical foot and that it needs to be a certain order of the iambus and anapest if done properly. Variations on this article are printed by the hundreds by organizations or by commercial firms. The point is that these are language arts, geography, sound games, or gimmicks; they have nothing to say about the voice behind the poem, or even how to try to find it.

Teaching poetry demands an involvement on the part of the teacher, a commitment to elicit the feelings or experiences of the student set down into something that may approach, but not yet be, a poem. Are we so afraid to tell our children that they are not poets, that they are only beginning to learn something of the craft, but that, if they wish, through work and rewriting, they may eventually achieve something of which they will be proud? I don't know about the children you teach, but I have enough respect for the young people with whom I work to know that they are amazingly aware when they have done a poor piece of work—that they cry out for praise when it is deserved, but that they know jolly well when they have copped out.

My own way of teaching is not done with fill-ins or gimmicks; it is done with a journal to be written in at home, walks and observations, trips, bringing objects of interest into the classroom, chalk and a chalkboard, praise for the good things, improvement for the bad, and most important, models of good poetry. Good poetry is read at the beginning of each class and oftentimes at the end. Students are given anthologies that include everything from Mother Goose to e. e. cummings, anthologies that are taken home or shared if children find a particular poem they wish to read to others.

This brings me to another important point, and that is the very deep concern I have for what we are giving our children as models of poetry. Charlotte Huck has said:

> Essential to learning to read and write is a rich environment of language opportunities. . . . The best preparation for school is to "bathe him [the child] in language" from his earliest days. . . . But many of our teachers do not see the

significance of integrating the language arts. They flock to reading meetings so they can learn more about the *skills* of teaching reading. . . . Little attention is given to children's purposes for reading or their desire to read for meaning. . . . Those of you who are interested in composition know that this is equally true about children's writing. Children need to have authentic writing experiences in order to produce careful observation and honest feeling.

I am certain we know that many of the children who come into our classrooms are not "bathed in language" from their earliest days; many do not even know Mother Goose, and I myself have discovered that as early as first grade I can instantly tell by children's writing if they have been given good literature or simply poor books that masquerade as literature at home. I know from the experience of having my poems reprinted in primers and textbooks over the years that any joy the child might find in reading a poem that I, or any other poet, has written is quickly apt to be dispelled by questions such as: "Why did the poet use a capital here?" "What word rhymes with 'ear'?" "Where did the poet put a question mark and why?" as well as questions about the poem even I can't answer. Perhaps these teachers' aids and workbooks are necessary, for it is possible that I am some sort of idealist who has far more faith in teachers than many educators. I secretly hope that the teacher will simply skip the questions and allow children to just enjoy a poem. If they can only apprehend its meaning in the early grades, so much the better. There is plenty of time later to truly comprehend, for even at my age I find myself still searching to comprehend the meaning of many poems and simply wallow about delightedly in apprehension. Is it any wonder that Louis Simpson has told us that poetry is castrated in the high schools? It is similarly dealt with at a much lower level.

"To teach literature," George Steiner tells us in his magnificent book *Language and Silence*, "as if it were some kind of urbane trade, of professional routine, is to do worse than teach badly. . . . To teach it as if the critical text were more important, more profitable than the poem, as if the examination syllabus mattered more than the adventure of private discovery, of passionate digression, is worst of all."

I deem these words as important to a teacher as the Hippocratic oath to a doctor; the right to the adventure of private discovery and passionate digression is too often taken away from the child or young person. But it follows that too often what the student is given to read as a model is not even worthy of attention. This turns children off, as well it should. We do not respect their intelligence, their ability to enter into the world of imagination as we should.

The crux of the matter is that I am upset when I hear a teacher using James Whitcomb Riley or Eugene Field or other versifiers of sentimentality and cuteness, when we have available to us so many outstanding anthologies compiled for young people, and a wealth of good poets of the past and present whose work, either written with the child in mind or for all ages, offers children good models written in a diction to which they can relate and consonant with their emotional and intellectual experience.

I must say again that the most disturbing thing of all to me is that in reading much, but certainly not all, of the material offered as a spur to writing with children, I have found that a large percentage of teachers and Poets-in-the-

Schools do not even use good poetry as models. I am a believer, as an anthologist, in reading only the best, but I have been shocked to discover that many of these poets, as well as teachers, are offering the work of other children as models: such books as *Miracles*, or such magazines as *Stone Soup*, or the booklets put together by the children in the classroom. *Miracles* is a book for adults, not for children; it tells adults what they want to hear, what they think children should be writing about—lovely nature themes and the like. *Stone Soup* is the product of inexperienced college students who, for all of their enthusiasm about the writing of children, know little about the subject, and have even had the audacity to publish a guide explaining to teachers and parents how to use their magazine as a model for would-be young writers. Would we take a child to the recital of a local piano teacher to hear music well played, or would we take him to hear Horowitz or play a recording of Rubinstein? Would we, in fostering art, point out the beauty of elementary-school drawings, or more wisely take our chldren to a museum or offer them a book of drawing and painting by the masters?

Some Poets-in-the-Schools have told me, and I have heard it from other teachers, that either the work of that poet is offered or there is no poetry at all—they simply tell the child to write, which gives rise—for me, at least—to doubts about the validity of the program, for I have seen what these children produce on photocopied sheets, in vanity and trade publications. I am not saying that of the $740,000 allocated to this program for one year some money did not go to some fine poets, working, dedicated to the principles that Ruth Whitman and Harriet Feinberg, in their handbook *Poem-Making: Poets in Classrooms,* espouse: ". . . the process is always more important than the product. . . . We did not intend to make poets out of students, but rather to create a new generation of poetry lovers, of children sensitive to their own common experience and its relation to literature—in short, a new generation of humanists."

These are admirable goals, and there are many Poets-in-the-Schools working toward these ends. But there are also those who do not see the consequences inherent in exposing children to people who may proclaim themselves poets, who deem themselves qualified because they have published their own work, or are so puffed up with pride over their own work that they hold it up as a model of what poetry should be and extract from their students the same sort of "spillage of raw emotion," as Ciardi would say. There are those who will accept anything, who are afraid to tell children that they are just beginning, who feel that criticism or revision destroys creativity, that all children are born poets, that no child should be given the right to fail, and that it is easy to write a poem if the proper gimmicks or tricks are provided.

These are dangers, and the remedies must be provided by you, the teachers, vigilant always for signs of any of this creeping, ever so silently or noisily, into your class-rooms. And even though you might be fortunate enough to have the finest of the Poets-in-the-Schools visit your class-room, their influence will be lost if you do not maintain that atmosphere that will always provide and uphold the same high standards for the writing of poetry as for any other pursuit, the "adventure of private discovery, passion-ate digression" and what George Steiner calls "humane literacy."

In Act II, Scene 2 of *Hamlet*, there is a conversation among Hamlet, Rosencrantz, and Guildenstern. We might read this passage for its parallel with Hamlet's own state of mind, his knowledge of a dangerous situation in the court, and his own vacillation and inability to act in the face of difficulties. But we might also look at it as a summing-up of the situation we have been examining: children applauded for their work as so-called poets and the consequences thereof.

Hamlet has summoned a troupe of strolling players to perform at court, hoping thus to expose his stepfather, and asks Rosencrantz about the players:

HAMLET

Do they hold the same estimation they did when I was in the city? are they so followed?

ROSENCRANTZ

No, indeed, are they not.

HAMLET

How comes it? do they grow rusty?

ROSENCRANTZ

Nay, their endeavour keeps in the wonted pace; but there is, sir, an eyrie of children, little eyases, that cry out on the top of the question and are most tyrannically clapped for 't; these are now the fashion and so berattle the common stages—so they call them—that many wearing rapiers are afraid of goose-quills, and dare scarce come thither.

HAMLET

What, are they children? who maintains 'em? How are they escoted? Will they pursue the quality no longer than they can sing? will they not say afterwards, if they should grow themselves to common players,—as it is most like, if their means be no better,—their writers do them wrong, to make them exclaim against their own succession?

ROSENCRANTZ

Faith, there has been much to do on both sides, and the nation holds it no sin to tarre them to controversy; there was for a while no money bid for argument unless the poet and the player went to cuffs in the question.

HAMLET

Is 't possible?

GUILDENSTERN

O, there has been much throwing about of brains.

HAMLET

Do the boys carry it away?

ROSENCRANTZ

Ay, that they do, my lord: Hercules and his load too.

Hamlet wishes to know who will win: those falsely praised, high-voiced children who, in later life, will censure those who should have held them in check by correct teaching of their craft, or those who demand that some order be restored, that the dangers be made manifest and met, lest the very order of all things be threatened. He asks this in light of his own situation, just as we may ask it of ours.

POETS OF THE
CHILD'S WORLD

Edward Lear:
A Legacy of Hope

The search for symbolic meaning in the work of Edward Lear, the Victorian painter and nonsense writer, often seems as amusing and bewildering as the sea voyage of the Jumblies. Supported by psychoanalytical, philosophical, and sociological findings, twentieth-century scholars incline toward theories that occasionally read more like the critics' own inventions than Lear's limericks and story poems. Thomas Byrom, in *Nonsense and Wonder: The Poems and Cartoons of Edward Lear*, views "The Owl and the Pussy Cat" as "alienation" in a "queer and dislocated landscape." To John Lehman, author of *Edward Lear and His World*, "The Dong with a Luminous Nose" is a "macabre Romantic fantasia" with a chorus that emphasizes "the Dong's desolation and sense of abandonment." What these and other treatises regrettably lack, for the most part, is an inquiry into the more crucial exploration of the reasons as to why children—who know nothing of symbolism—respond with *laughter* to the Owl and the Dong; why, indeed, Lear's limericks, alphabets, story poems, and drawings afford joy, rather than pain, to the young.

It is true that the circumstances of Edward Lear's life shaped both his drawing and writing; the background is fascinating, the inquiries fruitful. It is essential that the researcher recognize that Lear's love for birds stemmed from his early work as an ornithological draftsman; that suffering from bouts of epilepsy, asthma, and rheumatism, he left the "smoky-dark Londonlife" to begin his incessant travels; that he detested physical violence, torpidity, and all persons who embodied these traits. But the first children who listened to his "nonsenses," before he was twenty-five years old, and those whom he later met and for whom he drew and wrote his alphabets and story poems, had no need to know about Lear's life to respond to the Old Man with a Beard or a

> Pidy,
> Widy,
> Tidy,
> Pidy
> Nice insidy,
> Apple-pie!

The levels on which literature is read—for Lear has survived while other nonsense versifiers have perished—determine, without doubt, the extent to which readers may return countless times and read anew. Lear is as fresh today as a century ago, and new insights into his melancholy and depressions, his ambivalence toward the "great folk" that supported him physically but stifled him emotionally, are always revealing. If the Owl was able to take along "plenty of money," the researcher recognizes this as a fantasy of the man who was constantly setting up "eggzibissions" of his drawings and paintings to support himself and finance yet another of his journeys. In 1861, writing from St. Leonard's-on-Sea, Lear describes how he spent his days and evenings "prowling in the dark along the melancholy sea. . . ." Lear's acute sensitivity about his unattractive nose and poor eyesight, coupled with his fruitless hope to marry, is echoed in "The Dong with a Luminous Nose":

> And now each night, and all night long,
> Over those plains still roams the Dong; . . .
> While ever he seeks, but seeks in vain,
> To meet with his Jumbly Girl again;
> Lonely and wild, all night he goes,—
> The Dong with a luminous Nose!

But what do children find when they hear about the Dong? What they see in the sketch Lear drew for his story poem is a strange figure with an elongated body, buttons about his trousers, playing a "plaintive pipe." On his face is

> a wondrous Nose, . . .
> Of vast proportions and painted red,
> And tied with cords to the back of his head.
> In a hollow rounded space it ended
> With a luminous lamp within suspended,
> All fenced about
> With a bandage stout
> To prevent the wind from blowing it out;
> And with holes all round to send the light
> In gleaming rays on the dismal night.

Certainly this Dong is akin to the spacemen of Halloween, the battery-illuminated whirlygigs worn by children going out to trick-or-treat, shedding light on the "Bong-tree" that grows in their own neighborhoods. What the Dong may mean to them is probably

> A lonely spark with silvery rays
> Piercing the coal-black night,—
> A Meteor strange and bright:

and if it "wanders, pauses, creeps,—/Anon it sparkles, flashes, and leaps"; the vividness of the late-night vision can be as compelling as Martian men flashed on the television screen. Surely the invented place names, the humor of the Gromboolian Plain and the Hills of the Chankly Bore, the Jumblies landing "at Zemmery Fidd/Where the Oblong Oysters grow," and the anapestic rhythms override the use of the letter *o*, whose mournful sounds fascinate as Lear speaks of the "long, long clouds" and the "cruel shore." This is the stuff of poetic craftsmanship, the accompaniment to Lear's narrative. Children, as Paul Hazard observed, take what is needed. They have not the heart or time to read into the Dong, or indeed any of the story poems, the suffering of the lonely bachelor wandering along a plain or a rocky shore; the melancholy Lear calling, as in "Calico Pie," to the little birds or mice or fish who "never came back"; the Pobble who through ridiculous advice loses his toes.

How is it possible that children laugh at a succession of story poems and limericks wrested from the frustrations and problems that beset Lear? How can the brooding lines, the falling rhythms, fail to work their spell on children? The obvious answer is, of course, that because children have a "universal" and "consistent aversion" to "carefully established reality," as Kornei Chukovsky has noted, they will gladly subscribe to anything that overturns or attacks reason. Nonsense, in whatever form, drawing or words, is the escape hatch from the trials of life; it is lawless, it is innocent, and at its very best it is made by a rational, logical mind that knows the parameters of its power. It is essential, for example, that the Dong be a *dong* and not a man, for both adult and child would weep with a human who loses his Jumbly Girl. At the moment in which the reader cares what happens, in which empathy or sympathy are aroused, nonsense vanishes. And although the Dong and Uncle Arly totter dangerously on the brink of reality, Lear, always in control, has orchestrated with the greatest care. The Dong wears a ridiculous contrivance on his nose; Uncle Arly, although he dies in the end, has a pea-green cricket that settles on *his* nose. Both noses, as it happens, deeply meaningful to the scholar, are the stuff that children merely find ridiculous. They do not think of Lear's sensitivity about his ugly, shapeless nose. And so, for over a century, they have laughed!

The genius of the nonsense writer, and Lear in particular, is that he can attack reason through a variety of forms and narratives and drawings, each in tension and balance with each other. Lear recognized that there were many "sagacious persons" who objected to the "perversion of young folks' perceptions of spelling and correct grammar" in his work. He writes of Madame de Bunsen's contention that "she would never allow her grandchildren to look at my books, inasmuch as their distorted figures would injure the children's sense of the beautiful." In the 1960s many parents likewise frowned on Sendak's wild things as much too frightening for young children.

Lear's limericks run the gamut from mere silliness—the

old man who made tea in his hat, the old person who rode on the back of a bear, the old lady who taught little ducklings to dance—to what, in the real world, could only be construed as violence:

> There was an Old man with a gong,
> Who bumped at it all the day long;
>   But they called out, "Oh law!
>   You're a horrid old bore!"
> So they smashed that Old Man with a gong.

Several limerick characters die from gluttony, are drowned, and meet other dire ends. If scholars read into these deaths the happenings in Lear's life, or trace the changes in his attitudes from his earliest limericks to the last, the findings may be of interest. It is evident, however, that children do not comprehend, nor do they even apprehend, that the "they" of the limericks represents reason, convention, mediocrity, and Mrs. Grundy. Nor are they probably aware of Lear's dislike of noise, or the details of the drawing in which the Old Man's feet and legs are suspended a good twelve inches from the ground whereas the feet of the "they" (the solid citizenry) are planted on terra firma. All that the children find is the comeuppance, the knowledge that *anything is possible* in the nonsense world and it need not be of the highest moral order. Mischief, the antidote to convention and logic, also smashes the "great folk" and the "big folk" who are always sure of their responsibilities and their values. "You are so solid and distinct in going on constantly in doing what is right," Lear wrote to a friend; "I am so fluffy and hazy, and never know what is right and what isn't."

Here is the child speaking, the child in Lear, the child caught in a web of do's and don't's whose escape valve is the world of nonsense. Do children recognize that Lear's understanding was based on his own feelings about himself? At seventy-one years old he wrote in his diary that "Life today is happier than this child deserves. . . ." Oftentimes he spoke of himself as a child. He loved children and wished to "make little folks merry." If his own youth had been blighted, he was determined to offer joy to others, to lead them to escape from pain. While Lewis Carroll directly parodied Dr. Isaac Watts's "Against Idleness and Mischief" in "How doth the little crocodile," Lear chose another way, for he intensely disliked idleness both in his personal and writing life, but enjoyed mischief and made it incessantly, both with word distortion and drawing pen—and in his writing.

Upsetting the rational, reasonable order of the world and its humdrum patterns is consistent in the limericks, story poems, and drawings. The world of reality is off-limits. Each limerick character, each animal and bird, makes an escape in some fashion, sailing off to sea in odd contrivances, hopping the world three times round, accomplishing the impossible in any number of imaginative ways. The people of his drawings seldom touch earth; they fly, they sit in trees, they lie on tables, they dress in odd headgear, they eat inedibles, they effect ridiculous cures. Their bodies are, as Madame de Bunsen observed, distorted. Susan Hyman, author of *Edward Lear's Birds*, notes that "abnormalities of appearance are usually avian in character: frock coats stand out stiffly like tails, arms are flung back like vestigial wings, noses resemble beaks." For just as Lear invested his ornithological drawings with "a measure of his own whimsey and intelligence, his energetic curiosity, his self-conscious clumsiness and his unselfish charm," so did he turn the tables and give to his people both characteristics of bird and beast. It is not necessary that children know about Lear's work at London's Zoological Gardens or the menagerie at Knowsley. They have only to look at the drawings sketched for them to recognize that Lear has played broadly with both species, mixing up arms and wings, noses and beaks!

In a like manner he plays with words, inventing a Bong-tree, a Scroobious Pip, a "slobaciously" shining moon, toadstools that are "oribicular, cubicular and squambigular," and the marvelous choruses sung by Mr. and Mrs. Spikky Sparrow:

> Witchy witchy witchy wee,
> Twikky mikky bikky bee,
> Zikky sikky tee!

Many nonsense writers, of course, invent neologisms, employ alliteration, trade on anthropomorphism, and invest the inanimate with life. Many use anapestic, freewheeling rhythms and amusing sound patterns. But what others do not have is Lear's unique gift, and that gift is more than imagination, more than mischief and lawlessness, more than a blow to reason, order, and moral consequence. It is the gift that says not only is *anything* possible, but that there is *hope*. What happens in Lear is unique, for there is not a single limerick, story poem, or alphabet that does not offer this hope: an ape can tie up his toes in "four beautiful bows"; the old man will keep ringing until someone answers the bell. Hope reaches its quintessence and is stated more directly in the story poems. An Owl and a Pussy Cat, normal enemies in the real world, can sail 'away with plenty of food and money and music, buy a ring, marry, and dance by the light of the moon. That Lear thought of himself as an impecunious owl, that he could never summon the courage to propose to Gussie Bethell, is not important to the child. But that there is hope of escape and happiness is!

In "The Duck and the Kangaroo" the Duck recognizes that in order to leave his "boring life" in a "nasty pond," to entice the Kangaroo to the world beyond, he must be prepared for the objection that his feet are "unpleasantly wet and cold." He has already "bought three pairs of worsted socks" so both may travel in comfort as they go "To the Dee, and the Jelly-Bo-Lee" and hop "the whole world three times round." The Daddy Long-Legs and the Fly similarly flee from a world where the length of their legs is not acceptable. The Nutcracker and the Sugar-Tongs, aware of their "stupid existence," gallop off with the sole observation that they "will never go back any more!" All have found a way to fulfill their desire for a better life.

There are others who go in search of adventure and return home content that their whims have been satisfied, that an outing has given some new perspective. The Broom, the Shovel, the Poker, and the Tongs find that a drive in the park helps to alleviate the gloom of the dark and softens their anger toward each other. Mr. and Mrs. Spikky Sparrow discover that a flight into town to buy "a Satin sash of Cloxam blue," slippers, a new gown, and a bonnet will make them look and feel quite "gallobious and genteel" and protect them forever from "cold and pain." The Jumblies sail off in a sieve and return from their voyage in twenty years with everything from "a pound of rice" and a "lovely Monkey with lollipop paws" to "forty bottles of Ring-Bo-Ree" with such tales of wonder to tell that those who welcome them back vow to go off and see the sights themselves. And despite the Chair's complaint to the Table that "we *cannot* walk," the Table is confident that "It can do no harm to try . . ."

> So they both went slowly down,
> And walked about the town
> With a cheerful bumpy sound
> As they toddled round and round.
> And everybody cried,
> As they hastened to their side,
> "See! the Table and the Chair
> Have come out to take the air!"

The outing is made and they both return, in spite of a small misadventure, to dine and dance upon their heads and toddle off to bed.

Hope is present even in the saddest of Lear's story poems. The Pelicans may never see their Daughter Dell again, but they still chorus:

> Ploffskin, Pluffskin, Pelican jee!
> We think no Birds so happy as we!
> Plumpskin, Ploshkin, Pelican jill!
> We think so then, and we thought so still!

The Yonghy-Bonghy-Bò and Lady Jingly Jones, though parted, may mourn for each other. The Pobble who has no toes still returns with his nose intact, and the Dong hopes to "meet with his Jumbly Girl again." The researcher

may read into "Mr. and Mrs. Discobbolos" with its cata-
strophic ending an echo of William Blake's *Songs of Innocence* and *Songs of Experience*. Lear holds up the other
side of the mirror; the world is filled with the discontented
and fraught with accident and peril. *Anything* is possible!
Those who cannot escape or do not wish to wander, like
the Quangle-Wangle, can attract others—who come to him—
if there is hope and imagination. The old man in the New
Vestments learns a lesson about unconventional behavior.
The greed or carelessness of limerick characters may result
in their demise. But those who make the most of their
long noses, those who are curious and even eccentric, are
a microcosm of the world as it is. Uncle Arly must die,
but not before he has enjoyed the benefits of his Railway-
Ticket, visited the "Tiniskoop-hills afar," enjoyed the company of his Cricket "Clinging as a constant treasure,—/Chirp-
ing with a cheerious measure," and gazed on "golden
sunsets blazing."

Lear excels in nonsense because the balance between
word and picture continually offers children the apprehension that while anything can happen—the Discobbolos tragedy, the "theys," and the drownings—there is comeuppance
for the disagreeable and hope for change. His childlike
optimism, in spite of his own sad childhood, prevailed.
Those who have followed him, who understand nonsense
and are clever in word invention, alliteration, rhythmical
patterns, and ludicrous situations, have never equaled Lear
because they have neglected to note this unique aspect of
Lear's genius. In imitation of Lear, Laura Richards's owl,
eel, and warming-pan go out together to call on the soap-
fat man, find him absent and turn "the meeting-house upside

down." Also "The Hornet and the Bee" (note the similarity between Lear's "Said the Chair unto the Table" and "Said the bee unto the hornet") is a piracy of "The Courtship of the Yonghy-Bonghy-Bò." The hornet proposes to the bee, is refused in favor of a Cockychafer who marries the bee and eats her up. Shel Silverstein's "The Toad and the Kangaroo" involves a contentious discussion between two creatures arguing about names for their future children—Toadaroo or Kangeroad—who end up in disagreement and part. Silverstein ends with

> What a loss—what a shame
> Just 'cause they couldn't agree on a name.

Lear, more wisely, never moralizes. William Jay Smith's Floor and Ceiling separate in a rage when the Ceiling flies out the door leaving the house in ruins and the Floor alone. The Antimacassar and the Ottoman express a desire to leave a room they abhor with its ugly objets d'art but fail because they believe they can neither fly nor unpin themselves. Here there is no hope, no belief that the impossible can happen, no will to make a change, and perhaps, more poignantly, no remembrance that real friendship once experienced will sustain those who are left alone in their inevitable moments of sadness.

Children need not know of the great importance Lear placed upon his own friends, but they can certainly apprehend that even Uncle Arly had his Cricket:

> Never—never more,—oh! never,
> Did that Cricket leave him ever,—
>   Dawn or evening, day or night;—

Even the Yonghy-Bonghy-Bò and Lady Jingly Jones once knew happiness together; even the Dong harbors hope that he will find his Jumbly Girl and relive the joyous moments. Even Mr. and Mrs. Discobbolos once had a secure and happy home, and contentment. But those who have never known the pleasure of friendship have little. Friends who must part or leave each other in anger without the sustaining memories are blighted forever.

Will lesser nonsense charm the children of a century from now? This is but a researcher's idle speculation. What is perceived is that the work of Lear has survived not only because it attacks reason but because it portrays, both graphically and through musical language, the timeless dream of children to make great escapes, to enlist their imaginations in believing that in spite of elongated noses or foreshortened legs, ridiculous behavior or disastrous circumstances, action of some sort is preferable to apathy and idleness. There is a world beyond, Lear seems to tell the children, where I will take you, where anything and everything is possible. I have given you and drawn for you a Bong-tree, an owl who plays upon a guitar, a duck with worsted socks, the Jumblies and their seafaring sieve. And you laugh, and through that laughter grow and recognize that the nonsense abiding in the real world can be overcome by your belief in yourself and your imagination. And the children listen.

David McCord:
The Singer,
The Song,
and The Sung

It is an uncommon man who can remember, extract, and discern the best of the past, reshape and apply it to the present, and in the process offer others a generous share of his unique celebration of life.

David McCord is such a man: a poet who has not only given to Cambridge, Boston, and academe his myriad talents but during the past three decades produced a body of work that ranks highest among all poetry written for children in this country. John Ciardi has put it well: "One is too few of him and there is, alas, no second."

There is no second because there is no other American poet who understands, as does David McCord, the high and low points in the English and American tradition of poetry for the young. He is keenly aware of the contributions made by Isaac Watts, William Blake, Edward Lear, Lewis Carroll, Robert Louis Stevenson, Walter de la Mare, Elizabeth Madox Roberts, and others. It is one thing, of course, to be aware of and to comprehend a historical perspective, but quite another to translate this into one's own writing.

There are many who emulate or imitate the poets of the past. This is not difficult.

What is herculean is to assimilate this past and bring to it the unique voice that characterizes meaningful poetry. David McCord has done this. But he has also cherished, related to, and recalled his own childhood. He has absorbed the sights, sounds, wonders, tastes, and rhythms that have marked his life. The result has been poetry for children, uniquely American, punctuated and crafted with the speech patterns, the rhythms, and the "abiding faith in laughter" of today's children. His understanding of and respect for the sensitivities, interests, emotions, and thoughts of the child coupled with his own abiding curiosity and wonder are what distinguish his work and set him apart from others.

To view David McCord in historical perspective is to recognize that although he has rejected the moral didacticism of Isaac Watts, he is mindful that a child responds to a regular rhythm and rhyme in remembering poetry and that there is verse from which children can learn. He is eager to impart information. It may be facts as mundane as what a chicken eats ("Plymouth Rocks, Of Course") or the habits of the newt. It may be an amusing approach to the use of correct pronunciation, punctuation, and spelling in such poems as "You Mustn't Call It Hopsichord" or "Spelling Bee." In "Books" he writes:

> You exist? Want to *be*?
> Not with comics, cheap movies, commercial TV.

There may be an occasional warning—not to trust "[s]ly Mr. Halloween" and to be careful in using the word "only"; lessons in how to draw a monkey; and instructions in looking at snowflakes. His poems describe everything from fifty legs of a centipede to hornets' nests, fishing, and how to write verse. What rescues all this from being moralistic, didactic, and encyclopedic is his ability to present his enthusiasms and discoveries with respect for the child's intelligence as well as his glorious wordplay.

> Never talk down to a glowworm—
> Such as *What do you knowworm?*
> *How's it down belowworm?*
> *Guess you're quite a slowworm.*
> No. Just say
>
> >*Helloworm!*

Understanding of the child's point of view—the legacy of Stevenson—is of concern to David McCord. In "No Present Like the Time" there is not only wordplay but a confrontation with false morality:

> "Don't waste your time," they say. Waste time you will:
> And such as you wish, of course, is yours to squander.
> Don't call it wasted when you climb a hill!
> Through fields and woods to wander
>
> Is to be young. . . .

This attitude, of course, was also characteristic of William Blake and Lewis Carroll, both of whom believed that time spent in dreaming, play, and laughing is the right of the child. Here David McCord is at one with Blake and Carroll in reacting to the preachments of Watts. The sluggard is not to be viewed with total distaste; one does not have to be continually working like the busy bee who improves "each shining hour." In his poem "Make Merry" McCord is very close to Blake's nurse in "Songs of Innocence":

> Merry child, make merry!
> The sound of laughter dies
> So quickly, so contrary
> Are the wayward cloudy skies.

Like Blake, McCord recognizes the false nurse in "Songs of Experience" who admonishes the children, "Your spring and your day/Are wasted in play."

In "The Adventure of Chris" the point is evident. Chris's geography book

> for telling me
> what not to miss
> on Earth

elicits a quick reply from Toad, who wonders if the book says not to miss the flower bed, the pond, and

> Things under things—
> like slimy slugs, like
> bugs with wings.

The arithmetic book Chris carries does not impart the stuff of Toad's eating things alive and undivided, nor does it count the hops around the yard. The spelling book says nothing about a "good rainy spell."

McCord's intention in "Far Away" about the need for play is paramount.

> How far, today,
> Is far away?
> It's farther now than I can say,
> It's farther now than you can say,
> It's farther now than who can say,
> It's very *very* far away:

> You'd better better better play.
> You'd better stay and play today.
> Okay . . . okay . . . okay.

There is more to this poem, however, than a reaction to the moralism of Watts, a kinship with Blake and Carroll, the mystery of de la Mare, or the everyday world of Stevenson and Elizabeth Madox Roberts. It is one of the great number of poems that bear the stamp of David McCord's curiosity and wonder, his belief that apprehension is as important as comprehension, his intuitive understanding of rhythm as a force to carry forth the meaning of the words. Most important, it contains a pragmatism and an outlook that are totally American and a vernacular that emphasizes that practicality. It is curiosity that begins this particular poem, the cadence of which is brief and childlike. Other poems— "Breakfast," "Easter Morning," and "Conversation"—are but a few that also begin with questions.

"Take Sky" names words and sounds but ends on a note that permeates all of McCord's writing—"Man's *first* word: wonder . . . wonder. . . ." David McCord is always wondering—about leaves, words, and birds; and about things heard: the sound of trains, clocks, owls, birds, bells, and the elements. In "August 28" he combines interest in both shape and sound:

> A flock of swallows have gone flying south;
> The bluejay carries acorns in his mouth.
> I don't know where he carries them or why.
> I'm never sure I like the bluejay's cry,
> But still I like his blue shape in the sky.

His curiosity and wonder extend to the shape and sound of words. Here he ranges from the intensely cerebral to the most outrageously nonsensical. Echoes of Edward Lear can be felt in "LMNTL," where he writes, "We've hrd a brd, grls gigl"; in "Pome," "a nash a noak anna napple tree"; and in "Z," "When all is zed and done." Simpler to understand for younger children are his "Scat! Scitten!" or "Just Because . . ." in which

> Kittens have paws they don't have pawses,
> Lions have maws they don't have mawses.

Word games such as "Inside Information" preserve a Carrollinian ring:

> Debbie is in DEBt.
> You see her? DEB—B plus a *t*?

He also enjoys making up odd names—Shadwell Presswood Leeds, Mingram Mo, or Tiggady Rue. Most fascinating of all is "Dr. Klimwell's Fall," for it is Dr. I Klimwell (*I climb well*—if one is not reading too much into the name) who falls down and must climb up again to view all the wonders of the world. In this very long poem, based on Emerson's quotation "We wake and find ourselves on a stair; there are stairs below us . . . there are stairs above us, many a one, which go upward and out of sight," David McCord sounds a recurring theme of ascension and discovery. This appears in "Five Chants" ("Every time I climb a tree") and in "Up the Pointed Ladder," where the climb reveals countless wonders. Noticing everything about him is also felt in "The Walnut Tree," in which the poet recognizes

> That the world begins in the sweep of eye,
> With the wonder of all of it more or less
> In the last hello and the first goodbye.

It is the wonder, too, that sustains apprehension, for McCord well understands that questions cannot always be answered. This is most clearly felt in a poem such as "Queer":

> I seem to see
> in the apple tree,
> I seem to know
> from the field below,
> I seem to hear
> when the woods are near,
> I seem to sense
> by the farmer's fence,
> I seem to place
> just the faintest trace,
> I seem to smell
> what I can't quite tell,
> I seem to feel
> that it isn't real,
> I seem to guess
> at it, more or less.

and certainly is felt in the title poem in his book *Away and Ago*, which begins:

> Away and ago
> has the sound of over
> the hills and far
> away, but the rover
> hasn't returned yet
> for telling us what
> it was that he met
> with, or whether he got
> there at all, or indeed
> where it was that he chanced
> to be choosing. . .

"John," "Old Tim Toole," "There," and "I Have a Book" may be read on the same level. One can guess that they are autobiographical in nature, as is "The Walnut Tree," "Dr. Klimwell's Fall," and "Up the Pointed Ladder." Their quality is haunting.

> Up the pointed ladder, against the apple tree,
> One rung, two rungs, what do I see?
> A man by the roadside, his eye on me.
>
> Two rungs, three rungs, and so much higher:
> I see five miles to the white church spire.
> Bet you that man there wishes he were spryer.
>
> Three rungs, four rungs, holding on tight;
> Up near the apples now and ready for a bite.
> The man by the roadside—is *he* all right?
>
> Four rungs, five rungs—scary, oh my!
> There's not much left but the big blue sky,
> The faraway mountains, and a wild man's cry.
>
> Five rungs, six rungs. I guess I'm through.
> I seem a little dizzy but the apples are too.
> And the man yells "Sonny!" and the cow goes "Moo!"
>
> Seven rungs, eight rungs—I can't climb these.
> The wobble's in the ladder, it isn't in my knees.
> The man cries "Steady boy!" And up comes a breeze.
>
> Up comes a breezy "Now you come down slow!"
> I offer him an apple, but he just won't go.
> Well, it's all like that in the world below.

In this highly symbolic poem the reader discovers the boy climbing a ladder, ostensibly for apples. Mindful that he is being watched, that there is danger, he still continues his ascent. Both church spire and pointed ladder emphasize this upward thrust. The view is spellbinding, yet he cannot escape from the watchful eye of tradition, of the mundane world below. Stubbornly he refuses to remain earthbound, dependent on others. No matter how wobbly the ladder, he will hold his place, cherish his view and the literal fruit of his climb. It is the man below who is wild, who may not be "all right," who cannot understand what it is he seeks, and who wishes him to return to the safety of earth. The theme is repeated in another poem, "Song."

> Wind and wave and star and sea,
> And life is O! a song for me.
> Wave and wind and sea and star,
> Now I shall tell them what we are.
> Star and sea and wind and wave,
> I am a giant, strong and brave.
> Sea and star and wave and wind,
> You are the tiger I have skinned.

These two poems, among others, would seem to be David McCord's invitation to the young. One must set goals, climb for the apple, skin the tiger, and somehow make others understand that each individual must aspire to more than the "world below." A boy on a wobbly ladder may become a giant, uncertainty may become certainty—or conversely, certainty may become uncertainty. Refusal to settle for safety or mediocrity, to dream and to climb are the prerogative of youth or of anyone whose sensitivities are attuned to the discoveries of life. There will always be apprehension and more to engage our wonder and curiosity.

But if certain questions cannot be answered, there are others that can be dealt with in straightforward, everyday terms. Here is the pragmatic, practical poet pinpointing a grasshopper's fall ("The Grasshopper"), running a stick over the pickety fence ("Five Chants"), recognizing that one *should* have said a prayer ("Waltzing Mice"), making a list of what Santa Claus forgot last year ("A Christmas Package"), asking frankly "Why *Good*? What's Good?" about saying good-night, or drawing with pad and pencil.

The world is a very real place at times, and David McCord never forgets how matter-of-fact children can be. He keeps abreast of the world of TV, Laundromats, Little Leaguers, and Rapid Reading. He is alive to the current vernacular of "man alive," "natch," "the guy's name," "queer stinko stuff," "what's the diff?" "goshawful," and "real fast." An avowed admirer of the poet Elizabeth Madox Roberts for her ability to speak in the language of childhood, David McCord equals and often surpasses her. In "Wishful" the house is "flittery with bats." In "Bridges" he writes "[t]he big one dizzies me." Nor is any reader likely to forget "The Star in the Pail," in which the reflection "silvered in the water."

In a piece titled "Until I Was Ten" the poet recalls his early years. "I was fascinated," he wrote, "by the sight and sound and shape of everything that moved with rhythm. I was fascinated by everything that had a special motion or made a special noise. For rhythm, not rhyme, is the basis of poetry." It was family members who "made me feel I was not alone in loving the sound of words and the rhythm of words put together in the right order."

Certainly he is a master of rhythm. The lyricism of "The

Walnut Tree" carries the reader along in backward and forward surges.

> There was once a swing in a walnut tree,
> As tall as double a swing might be,
> At the edge of the hill where the branches spread
> So it swung the valley right under me;
> Then down and back as the valley fled. . . .

"The Star in the Pail" combines the hush of coming evening, the quiescence of nature with the contrasting rhythmic pattern of a commonplace errand:

> When evening slippered over like the moth's brown wing,
> I went to fetch the water from the cool wellspring.

The carefully crafted rhythms of "Song" and "Suddenly" attest to an ear alive to the rhythms of nature and of skating in wide sweeps. The choice of trochaic dimeter for the disaster in "Marty's Party" must be the envy of any poet.

> Marty's party?
> Jamie came. He
> seemed to Judy
> dreadful rude. He
> joggled Davy,
> spilled his gravy,
> squeezed a melon
> seed at Helen.

And the humorous anapestic beat of "Bananas and Cream" is a natural source of laughter:

> Bananas and cream,
> Bananas and cream:

> All we could say was
> Bananas and cream.

The iambic lilt of his story poems as well as the straightforward iambus of his informative verse are, indeed, "the right order." The lugubrious dactyl, in combination with the trochee, is a brilliant choice for a poem about castor oil.

> Ever, ever, not ever so terrible
> Stuff as unbearable castor oil.

There is no precedent for McCord's sure sense and choice of rhythm; he is unequaled.

His use of figurative language is unaffected and wise. He does not burden young readers with overemphasis on poetic devices. Personification occasionally appears. After the fashion of Lear he tells the story of "Dr. Ping and Mr. Pong." In "Whistle" a Mother Diesel train worries that young Whistle will not blow. Leaves talk through all the seasons in the poem called "Leaves"; and the sun in "The Firetender"

> rises from the dead of night
> And rakes the star-coals up the sky

and later

> watches the reflection spread,
> Then banks the fire and goes to bed.

An imaginary battle characterizes "In Winter Sky":

> Late afternoon: clouds made a hole.
> Sun put two fingers through and stole
> The golden tops of three or four
> Big trees. He would have stolen more;
> But clouds, not liking what he did,
> Closed up the hole and clapped a lid

On all the trees that they could sight.
Sun whipped his swords out for a fight,
Slashed into them. Each blade he thrust
Shone like a stairwell full of dust
With crosslight on it. Lots of trees
Held up their fiery shields to these.
The clouds, now cut to ribbons, red
With evening blood, closed ranks and fled.

Alliteration is often handled with wit. In "Books Fall Open" the poet challenges the young reader:

What *might* you be,
perhaps *become*,
because one book
is somewhere? Some
wise delver into
wisdom, wit,
and wherewithal
has written it.

A bee in the poem "Hammock"

fills the air
With little flags and floats away

Assonance is presented deftly in "Cocoon," when the caterpillar

sleeps awhile before it flies
And flies awhile before it dies.

and in "Watching the Moon":

September evenings such as these
The moon hides early in the trees,
And when we drive along the shore

> I think I miss the trees the more
> Because the moon is coming down
> Beyond the branches and will drown.

Metaphor and simile are never overpowering. In "Ants and Sailboats" the poet matter-of-factly sees sailboats with

> The sails stuck up like tiny thumbs
> And fingernails. . . .
>
> Or stacked themselves like cards to bunch
> Beyond the islands.

In "Suddenly" we see

> the fields like dinner plates
> in the shine and the flash of the morning sun.

"Elm Seed Blizzard" pictures seeds flying loose like "tiny saucers without a cup." A row of machines in the poem "Laundromat" becomes "one train: a nice long rumbly kind of freight," and "Crickets" are, indeed, ticket-takers

> all busy punching tickets,
> clicking their little punches.

Onomatopoeia has never been livelier than in "Five Chants" ("The pickety fence"):

> Give it a lick
> Give it a lick
> Give it a lick
> With a rickety stick

and never more clearly presented to young people than in "Take Sky," where poet invites reader and listener to marvel at the great number of words whose very sound echoes their meaning:

Three words we fear but form:
Gale, twister, thunderstorm;
Others that simply shake
Are tremble, temblor, quake.
But granite, stone, and rock:
Too solid, they, to shock.

"No poet worth his salt," David McCord has written in
Pen, Paper and Poem, "has ever been able to write the
kinds of poems he wanted to write without a basic knowledge of meter, rhythm, rhyme and the established verse
forms." A poet may abandon rhyme and forms, "but he
will never abandon meter and rhythm." McCord has aban-
doned neither rhyme nor form. His rhymes, whether in
couplet, tercet, quatrain, or other patterns, not only sound
true but offer delightful surprises. Enjambment is frequently
used in conjunction with closed couplets with grace and
wit. "Alphabet (Eta Z)" ends with

23
Your twenty-three's
In wow! Xerxes
24
Shows X the core
Of twenty-four.
25
Y keeps alive
In twenty-five;
26
Z's in a fix:
Poor twenty-six!

Most amazing is the way in which McCord begins and
ends many of his poems, for they seem to spring to mind

almost as a part of the stream of consciousness. This he has acknowledged as a legacy from his mother, "who could always find the surprising word to express the surprising idea." "Three Signs of Spring" plunges in with "Kite on the end of the twine"; "Ducks Walking" opens with "Actually five"; and in "Take Sky" it is as if the reader or the listener were barging in on the poet's thoughts: "Now think of words. Take *sky*." But the most startling surprises are his endings. In a poem such as "That's Not," in which he explains the difference between grouse and pheasant, weasel and mink, hare and rabbit—information that could easily turn into a lesson—he writes:

> No rabbit *that*. No, sir! a *hare*:
> long ears, long legs. But not long where
> you're looking. Please learn not to stare.

"Alley Cat" is another apt example.

> His nightly song will scarce be missed:
> Nine times death claimed our alley cat.
> Good-by, you old somnambulist!—
> A long word, that.

The endings of "The Newt," "The Poultry Show," "Dividing," "Alphabet (Eta Z)," and "Snake" are but a few examples of deftly handled material that could easily, in another writer's hand, be ruined by a last line. In "Pumpkin Seeds" David McCord talks about carving a pumpkin. In the last two lines of the second stanza he tells us,

> We bring alive a thing that's dead,
> And do it with a sense of love.

It would be impossible for anyone to write *real* poetry for children without this sense of love for bringing things alive.

His poetry for the young is built on a strong foundation of literary tradition. Watts pointed the way toward remembering in rhyme, but the moral overtones and heavy-handedness of his preaching are no fare for today's children. Blake introduced the necessity for joy, dreaming, and play; Carroll, the cerebral content of words and games, in addition to joy. Lear and Carroll, the bachelor Victorians, introduced the value of nonsense and wordplay. Stevenson zeroed in on the everyday experience in the life of the child, de la Mare on the mystery. Roberts observed the American scene of childhood with an eye to people and events presented in the language of the child. Such a tradition is felt in many aspects of McCord's work.

What David McCord has added is the invitation to the young people of this country to look about, to be aware, to learn and grow, as he himself has done, with a keen eye and ear for the American landscape, its rhythms, its vernacular, and its subject matter from sky to earth and below. He has never lost the sensitivities of childhood, the love of children, or the knowledge that curiosity and wonder are the lifeblood of the young. His invitation is compelling. It cannot be ignored and is not cast aside, because children know that its messages is true, that its rhythms and surprises, laughter and wonder are theirs to seize.

In his second book for children, *Take Sky*, David McCord wrote an introductory poem:

> Blesséd Lord, what it is to be young:
> To be of, to be for, be among—

> Be enchanted, enthralled,
> Be the caller, the called,
> The singer, the song, and the sung.

Surely, David McCord is the singer whose songs will be sung as long as there are children to listen.

Nine Poets of the Child's World

HARRY BEHN (1898–1973)
The "Willingness to Wonder"

It is a fascinating and far-flung legacy that Harry Behn has left to the child reader and to those interested in literature for children, characterized, perhaps, by his own words: "Innocence is hardly more than a willingness to wonder." How unusual it is to think of Behn—born in Arizona when it was still a territory, educated at Harvard, and world traveled—as a man of innocence. And yet it is the right phrase, for his willingness to wonder and wander, his enthusiasms and curiosity moved within a changing world that he persisted in viewing, most often, through the eyes of the innocent.

His books, ranging from the child's poetic voice of *Windy Morning* through stories and novels and further poetry as well as translation of haiku, carry a thread of transcendentalism; it is the Indian Earth-Mother, the gods of the Sun People, the god Aplu, the rising of the sun, the "almost imperceptible experience of wonder, removed from knowledge." "When a child," he wrote in *Chrysalis*, "sees his first butterfly and becomes himself a flying flower, such innocence has in it more reality than any however heroic whiz around the planet." So it was that the language of a bug, a chicken, a crow, a storm, rain, or a train could spellbind him into poem or prose making.

Like Walter de la Mare he found elves and wizards, fairies and magical beings of whom to write; like Robert Louis Stevenson he became the child speaking in "Swing Song" or "Pirates." Yet his was an American heritage, rooted in world history. *All Kinds of Time* clearly expressed that

> Seconds are bugs
> minutes are children
> hours are people
> days are postmen
> weeks are Sunday School
> months are
> north
> south
> east
> west
> and in between
> seasons are
> wild flowers
> tame flowers
> golden leaves
> and snow
> years are
> Santa Claus
> centuries are
> George

> Washington
> and forever is God.

This and the poems within his other books of poetry for children are those of an American child and his particular wonder:

> Tell me, tell me everything!
> What makes it Winter
> And then Spring?

he asks through the child in "Curiosity." Yet the series of questions of the poem end with his own continuing questions.

> Tell me! or don't even grown-ups know?

This search, therefore, led him on. It was not unusual that because of his love for seasons and simplicity he should turn to the translation of Japanese haiku; that he should examine the life of a crow in *Roderick* or Dawn Boy, the Indian, in *The Painted Cave*; that his mother's childhood in Denmark should inspire him to write *The Faraway Lurs*; or that his questioning of the correlation between Etruscan and American civilization spun itself out in *Omen of the Birds*.

Poetry, he wrote, "must be presented with careful incompleteness of information." Incompletion thus sustains curiosity; information is not a raison d'être for the poet, and "willingness to wonder" is Harry Behn's unique contribution to children's literature.

JOHN CIARDI (1916–1986)
Beyond "Spillage of Raw Emotion"

It is one thing to write nonsense verse for children, as many do, with outrageously silly situations, concocted creatures, and humorous story lines as well as attention to contemporary concerns—but quite another matter when a poet, in command of his craft, puts his mind and heart to it. John Ciardi, whose background was that of a scholar, critic, and adult poet, was such a craftsman who kept in touch with the matters that delight the young and, through numerous books, presented them with a wealth of observations, creatures, and situations that derive their strength from pattern and rhyme that ring clear and true to the ear and often invite active participation and much laughter.

Ciardi's imagination was in tune with the young who enjoy the absurdity of ridiculous names; in a sense, he updated Edward Lear for the contemporary child with his "Brobinyak" who lives in the

> Forest of Foffenzee
> In the land of the Pshah of Psham,

where one might also meet "Radio Eels" or the "Banjo Tern" or the "Scrawny Shank," or the "Saginsack" whose

> Radio Horns
> And Aerials for ears

could "be listening to you." Again, in the story of "The Army Horse and the Army Jeep" there are echoes of the inanimate table and chair of Lear. Yet Ciardi was not imitating; he was his own man, unlike others writing for children who seize nonsense and preposterous names and situations and who do not, in craft or in use of symbol, measure up to Lear.

Ciardi's interest in animals—the shark, python, whale, crow, ape, boa constrictor, and others—permeates his books in an imaginative series of short story poems. Nature is also given emphasis in "How to Tell the Top of a Hill" or "The River Is a Piece of Sky." Ecological concerns crop up in "And They Lived Happily Ever After for a While," all of which focus on the same wonder and imaginative speculation as in "The Reason for the Pelican" or "Fast and Slow," in which the "fast young crow" does not know "Where to go."

The occasional cuteness of "Mummy Slept Late and Daddy Fixed Breakfast" or "Prattle," although these poems are popular, seems to me to show Ciardi at less than his best. The strength and haunting quality of

> There once was an Owl perched on a shed
> Fifty years later the Owl was dead.
>
> Some say mice are in the corn.
> Some say kittens are being born

prove his ability to soar beyond mere childishness.

In whatever form he chose to use, his control is always admirable; his couplets, tercets, quatrains, limericks, attest to his carefully constructed meter and rhyme; his technique is happily beyond what he himself called the "spillage of raw emotion." Ciardi wrote to entertain in a rhythm to which the young respond, and if occasional morals creep in now and again, they are done with a sophistication and humor that are so carefully worked into the poem that they cannot be faulted.

NORMA FARBER (1909–1984)
"Worn Like a Jewel"

It is the wonders and miracles of life that captured Norma Farber's imagination in her work for young people, a devotion to the seemingly obscure to which she held a glittering magnifying glass. This celebration of life is an unending invitation to marvel at both the commonplace and the extraordinary, brought into focus by startling metaphor and rich patterns of form and rhythm.

Nowhere is this more evident than in her poems of the Nativity—a theme she explored constantly in some of her finest work for adults. With tenderness she wrote of Joseph and Mary, of the Holy Child, the three kings, and the surrounding mysteries of one night almost two thousand years ago. But her mind leaped, as well,

> To think of all the kings who were not there,
> who never dropped their crowns and cares of state
> unceremoniously. . . .

For children she also turned "to think of those absent" in fresh and vivid imagery. Here are the sea creatures who could not make the journey, as well as the hibernators, animals, insects, and people who do. It is the ladybug who is

> Worn like a jewel
> a fiery pin,
> a ruby sequin

over the baby's heart, and the dove who asks

> What thing
> should I sing

> little king?
> *Coo-roo?*

Her use of synesthesia is remarkable in numerous poems, but reaches a pinnacle when the spider speaks to the Holy Child:

> I loop my wiring silver-clear,
> to light your manger chandelier,
> Listen! My web is what you hear.

In *Small Wonders*, creatures and objects, in varying poetic forms, force the reader to see and think anew. Maggots are transformed into "coral strings" or "grains of glistening rice." The caterpillar is a "concertina," the turtle a "creeping stone." A walnut becomes a tiny "wizened tot" in his cradle of shell, and a dandelion a "white pincushion." Leaves from a rich autumn tree fall as coins in "Spendthrift."

Farber's poetic craft enabled her to give readers a continual wealth of assonance, consonance, and alliteration, weaving in and out of rhythms through which her readers may listen to many a song unsung.

> Softer than the breath of woolly bears,
> sleeping;
> the sound of my velvet bellows,
> creeping.

begins the "Caterpillar Carol" in *Never Say Ugh to a Bug*, a collection that brings to life arresting portraits of the insect world mixed with humor. Wit and imagination are found in *As I Was Crossing Boston Common*, with its splendid refrain of "how uncommon" to the nonsense creatures who parade before the reader. Yet she is equally adept at the serious. In *How Does It Feel to be Old?* the woman tells a child who asks,

I'm dreaming the past
as though it never was over. . . .

Norma Farber's talents were far-ranging. She brought to the world of poetry written for children a gift of music and of observation, expanding horizons of reality and of fantasy. We are all the richer for her poetry.

RANDALL JARRELL (1914–1965)
"Somebody That Will Listen"

"The trouble isn't making poems," Randall Jarrell's little bat-poet bitterly says, "the trouble's finding somebody that will listen to them." Such an assertion, made by one of America's leading contemporary poets, gives rise to a series of speculations about Jarrell and his unique contribution to children's literature. For when reviewers hailed *The Animal Family*, the story of a lonely hunter who finds a mermaid, a bear, a lynx, and a boy who live together in understanding, it became apparent that joy and a happy ending are what make most readers comfortable.

In his first book, *The Gingerbread Rabbit*, Jarrell also devises a happily-ever-after. But here he was only wetting his feet. Elements of "The Gingerbread Boy" permeate this story for the very young; there is but one verse in the book, the call of the vegetable man hawking turnip greens (published in another form as an adult poem), and yet one can find all the embryonic themes that were used in his subsequent books—innocence, loneliness, the search for a home and fulfillment, fear, love, and forebodings of death.

These themes recur on a more poetic level in *The Animal Family*, *The Bat-Poet*, and *Fly by Night*, and these books, one suspects, will stir and elicit a response now and in future years in the most sensitive adults and children. For the reaction of many reviewers and critics, among these (most amazingly!) other poets, often makes it painfully clear that the entire point of what Jarrell has so beautifully done is completely misunderstood. These critics fail to recognize that they are the pompous, egotistical mockingbirds of *The Bat-Poet* who listen only to their own songs and voices, who do not hear the little bat crying out in loneliness, with a need to be heard, loved, protected, and accepted for his individual contribution. The hunter and mermaid of *The Animal Family* and David of *Fly by Night* represent, among others, those with this same loneliness and search. The knowledge that they are different from others, that growth is painful and love hard-won, takes a different turn in all three books; each character has his mentor, his own personality, and whether in human or animal form the fall from innocence is dealt with on various meaningful levels.

Jarrell drew from the animal world a symbolic level that deserves careful study. Is the owl of fear and possible death in *The Bat-Poet* any relation to the owl of security and mother love of *Fly by Night*? The symbols are many, and Jarrell explored them through beautiful prose and magnificent poetry. It is quite possible, one feels, that the lack of formal poetry in *The Animal Family* makes it a less formidable, more comfortable story for some readers.

As in his adult poetry, Jarrell was laying bare his own emotions in his work for children, and never more so than in *The Bat-Poet*, which is, to me, the most eloquent story ever written about the sensitivity and life of a poet, about pompous critics, or indeed about what the making of poems is all about.

X. J. KENNEDY (1929–   )
The Worlds of X. J. Kennedy

One of the worlds of X. J. Kennedy lies just next door in a neighborhood where mothers keep pet pigs, play slide trombones, and bake inedible pies while fathers conjure up a good whirl for their entire families in a concrete mixer. Through their houses pass an assortment of odd aunts, uncles, and grandparents, as well as a monstrous mouse who crashes a birthday party. It is a heady place where the Tooth Fairy, fabric shrinkers, and a birthday cake

> so full of eggs
> It cackles, clucks, and scratches

are part of everyday living; where salami subs, gumball machines, staplers, and cough drops enjoy a life of their own. It is, most important, a world where children may exercise their own imaginations to create still more fun.

> My mother's big green gravy boat
> Once thought he was a navy boat.
>
> I poured him over my mashed potatoes
> And out swam seven swift torpedoes.
>
> Torpedoes whizzed and whirred, and—WHAM!
> One bumped smack into my hunk of ham. . . .

Kennedy's imagination overflows with absurdities. Spaghetti, he writes, makes very unusual shoelaces. In winter one can prepare "Snowflake Souffle" by stirring it with "two hind legs," baking it in an igloo, and slicing it with a "rusty ice-skate." The Thrift-Rite Supermart provides enough frozen delicacies to whip up an "Instant Storm." A coat made of cocoa skin makes one feel "All warm and scummy."

His "Far-out Family" includes a great-great-grandma who sleeps in a treehouse, an Aunt Jill who insists that dill stalks will afford "sour puss" pickles "a few good tickles," and Cousin Carrée, who serves—both literally and figuratively—"a good square meal" including ground round shaped into bricks with hamburger buns squeezed into squares. His

> uncle, General Doug MacDougal,
> Sleeps nights inside a huge blue bugle.

while

> All four of my uncle Erics
> Tear their hair and throw hysterics.

In *Brats* Kennedy conjures up scores of annoying youngsters who are either victims or perpetrators of further hilarity:

> At the laundromat Liz Meyer
> Flung her brothers in the dryer.
> Round and round they've whizzed for years,
> Not yet dry behind the ears.

In addition to zany family situations that include household pets, there are "Unheard-Of Birds and Couldn't-Be Beasts" as well as attic ghosts and a variety of "Cheerful Spirits." Dinosaurs fascinate Kennedy, as do creatures of the sea. There is a limerick about a nervous sea captain from Cheesequake, and a rousing story poem about Mackerel Mack and Halibut Hal. Kennedy's lines sing:

> With walloping tails, the whales off Wales
> Whack waves to wicked whitecaps. . . .

In this, as in all of his work, Kennedy outshines mere versifiers with a superb use of rhyme, meter, onomatopoeia, alliteration, and delightful word play.

> The cows that browse in pastures
> Seem not at all surprised
> That as they moo they mow the lawn
> And their milk comes pasture-ized.

Digested by a giant snail, Uncle Artemus McPhail remarks
that he "finds this whole thing hardly moving." In his animal
alphabet, *Did Adam Name the Vinegarroon?*, he writes of
a Tyrannosaur:

> Yet tyrants, under Time's slow hand,
> Must one day bow their necks.
> Now in museums—bones wired—stand
> Tyrannosaurus wrecks.

Kennedy's work is rich in simile and metaphor:

> All day bats drowse in houses' eaves
> Like tents collapsed for storage,

a mole

> tunnels underneath your lawn
> To shoulder up a wrinkle,

and an iguana

> demonstrates the signs
> Of somewhat hasty wrapping.

While a good portion of Kennedy's early verse for children
in *One Winter Night in August* and *The Phantom Ice Cream*

Man appear as strictly nonsensical, there is, as in all excellent nonsense, a toehold on reality, a recognition of the human condition. Mothers may not buy "six paper swimming pools" or "backscratchers for a pig," but they do enjoy bargain sales. Mighty Mump cereal may not contain "sugar, corncobs, and dye," but televised, it is

> made up to look simply ethereal!

In his recent book of poetry *The Forgetful Wishing Well* lies Kennedy's other world of reality where sticky ice-cream cones, forbidden TV watching, excuses to stay up late, reactions to ugly deer statues, and even a child's poignant sense of loss are explored:

> I take my plastic rocket ship
> To bed, now that I'm older.
> My wooly bear is packed away—
> Why do the nights feel colder?

Humor remains keen, as in conversations between a crocus and an artichoke, a truck and a taxi. A school bus, window screen, fog, snow, and old stone mill are personified. But nonsense has been routed. In "Roofscape" one can see a skyscraper shadowing "A low-kneeling church," watch pigeons, traffic snarls, and the world as it is. An unforgettable use of onomatopoeia occurs in "Rain into River":

> Rain into river
> falling
>
> tingles
>
> one
> at

            a
            time
            the trout's
            tin shingles.

Kennedy's title poem, "To a Forgetful Wishing Well," sets
the tone:

    All summer long, your round stone eardrum held
    Wishes I whispered down you. None came true.
    Didn't they make one ripple in your mind?
    I even wished a silver pail for you.

X. J. Kennedy is at home in both worlds; to each he is
making a significant contribution.

EVE MERRIAM (1916–   )
"To Find Another Way"

Eve Merriam's versatility is astounding. A keen observer
of contemporary life, she brings to her poetry a fresh outlook
on all phases of the modern world, its delights as well as
absurdities. Agile and penetrating, she beguiles her readers
with a variety of rhythms, rhymes, and forms attuned to
the spirits of the young. Her craftsmanship is exemplary.

Merriam's themes range from the joy of words and wordplay through a gamut of observations about contemporary
life. Her concerns for humanity, ecology, and the quality
of life often find expression in the part played by poetry
itself with its possibilities for self-expression. What underlies
all her writing is the art of asking the child reader to extend
horizons, develop sensibility, cultivate curiosity, and become
aware of the creativity for both the individual and society.
"I cannot speak until you come," says a poem. "Reader,
come, come with me."

For the child who accepts this invitation and enters into
Merriam's work there will be the love of words and sounds
for their own sake. In her poem "Having Words" she lists
the things that the word "umbrage" is not, and tells
her audience: "You'll have to find out for yourself/ some-
day when you're having words." She plays with the alphabet, numbers, punctuation, the points of the compass,
and a myriad of other objects and ideas, always asking the
reader to join in the fun. Yet she warns against mediocrity.
A cliché, she explains,

> is what we all say
> when we're too lazy
> to find another way.

It is her unique talent that she is able to avoid didacticism
by playing a dual role as poet and reader. Writing of "it"
and "they," she comments that

> THEY just make it all up,
> and we go along.

By becoming part of the "we," she never points an accusing
finger at the child.

She can be delightfully caustic, attacking television and
its ridiculous commercials, the supermarket with its "banana
detergent" and "deodorant pie," plastic plants that "keep
us germ-proof and dirt-free," as well as the "neuter com-
puter" and the "cult" of bargain sales.

> You can take away my mother,
> you can take away my sister,
> but don't take away
> my little transistor.

Some of her finest writing is about people whose "independent voices" have wrought meaningful changes in the world—Frederick Douglass, Ida B. Wells, Elizabeth Blackwell and others. Her poems about poetry itself are memorable. In "How to Eat a Poem" she advises the reader to "bite in. . . ." The poem "is ready and ripe now, whenever you are." In "Reply to the Question: *How Can You Become a Poet?*" she suggests young writers observe the varying phases of the leaf in spring, summer, and autumn and

> then in winter
> when there is no leaf left
> invent one.

Eve Merriam's invitations to participate in both poetry and life are invitations that ring with anticipation and challenge. They are impossible to resist!

JACK PRELUTSKY (1940–   )
"An Ogre's Backbone, Slightly Smashed"

The work of Jack Prelutsky lies outside the province of classical light verse, which stresses wit, decorum, and elegance. The broader limits of contemporary light verse include wordplay and earthy humor, but even here his work eludes the category. What links him to the genre is his use of traditional form, a keen ear for lively rhythm, and a penchant for rollicking alliteration.

Prelutsky's verse is set apart by a fascination with the aberrations of human physiology and behavior, a taste for the macabre, and a curious delight in the gross and baser side of human nature. This is felt in his almost obsessive concern with gluttony and obesity, a greed that goes beyond familiar foods and dwells on a never-ending variety of nonedibles. Gretchen's pot contains

> A lizard's gizzard, lightly mashed,
> an ogre's backbone, slightly smashed.

The Wozzit eats clothes; Herbert Glerbett eats fifty pounds of lemon sherbet and turns into

> a thing that is a ghastly green,
> a thing the world has never seen,
> a puddle thing, a gooey pile,
> of something strange that does not smile.

Pies made of nuts and bolts, of shoe polish and candied eyeballs, are typical staples. Pumberly Pott's niece devours his automobile piece by piece. Many of Prelutsky's characters eat each other: the flonster, floober, flummie, and flakker, the frummick and frelly. Others squash each other by sheer force of overweight.

While all of this might be construed, by some, as nonsense, there is an element in the verse that goes beyond nonsense, for the reader is often threatened directly. The grobbles, It, lurpp, and preternatural creatures, Prelutsky warns, may also eat you. In *Nightmares: Poems to Trouble Your Sleep* and *The Headless Horseman Rides Tonight* a catalog of supernatural beings wallow in blood and death. The bogeyman will "crumple your bones in his bogey embrace," and the ghoul, having eaten other boys and girls, waits outside school "perhaps for you." Here are echoes of the German school, of *Struwwelpeter*, with cautionary tales to frighten, things that exist physically to attack beyond the limits of the page.

Rolling Harvey down the Hill is another instance of the darker side of human nature. Harvey is nasty, selfish, a cheat and braggart, a "tub of lard," a sadist who ties up his friends, and, although he is rolled down the hill for punishment, the reader learns that boys who dress neatly and "dumb" girls are outside of Harvey's accepted circle.

Prelutsky has some lighter moments with wordplay. In *The Sheriff of Rottenshot* there is a bicycling centipede who

> merits medals
> working all those centipedals

and an ocelot who likes to "toss a lot" and "fuss a lot." As a craftsman Prelutsky knows the power of the anapestic line, alliteration, and the fun of making up foolish names and unusual creatures.

For readers who feel that physical force, gluttony, and a dose of fear are funny, Prelutsky will serve well. But for those of differing sensibility, other light verse may hold more appeal.

SHEL SILVERSTEIN
The Quintessential Moralist

When Shel Silverstein, in 1974, offered children the prospect of venturing to the place *Where the Sidewalk Ends*, the invitation was irresistible. Here lay an opportunity for the young to defy danger signs, to peer over the edge of crumbling cement and discover a world where rhyme and picture engendered delight, where children might find their foibles, wishes, and hates mirrored by Silverstein in a manner that tradition and propriety, hitherto, suggested be kept private and unspoken.

Oh the thumb-sucker's thumb
May look wrinkled and wet
And withered, and white as the snow,
But the taste of a thumb
Is the sweetest taste yet
(As only we thumb-suckers know).

What a contrast to Dr. Heinrich Hoffman's "Little Suck-a-Thumb" in *Struwwelpeter*, whose thumbs were severed by the scissors man as punishment for the dreadful habit! Silverstein's appeal partially lies in the use of the pronoun "we," which instantly establishes him as an empathetic adult who is not above self-censure.

If reviewers were slightly nonplussed at Silverstein's occasional indelicacies in subject matter or overanxious to ferret out his derivativeness (usually, to my mind, incorrectly), the popularity that followed *Sidewalk*'s publication silenced most criticisms. By 1981 and the arrival of *A Light in the Attic*, readers gobbled up Silverstein with joy. He had, as one reviewer put it, become the "guru" of the poetry unit. His books of verse had come to occupy a place of honor in libraries, on home bookshelves, and in bookstores.

Silverstein's magnetism is not surprising to anyone in touch with children's feelings and their penchant for wild invention and hyperbole. What child could resist a verse about someone who loses his head—when the drawing be that it has been mistaken for a rock on which the headless someone sits? Who would not laugh at thirsty Jane, so lazy that she lies on her back with open mouth waiting for rain to slake her thirst? What is more surprising is that behind the *seemingly* silly verses, camouflaged in part by amusing pictures, breathes a twentieth-century moralist and didacticist who would gladden the heart of the eighteenth-century Dr. Watts and his followers. What is utterly astounding is that children, who normally shun didacticism in any form, accept it enthusiastically in Silverstein!

Since 1715, when the Reverend Isaac Watts published his *Divine and Moral Songs for Children*, a strain of high moralism has characterized poetry written for children. Edward Lear and Lewis Carroll were among the first who avoided didacticism, stressed hope, and advocated escape from mundane unpleasantries and the "theys" who stifled individualism. Both Lear and Carroll fought the concept of "PLEASURE'S wiles" with nonsense and parody. It remained for Robert Louis Stevenson to introduce the child in a garden that, albeit seeded occasionally with English chauvinism, established real play and actual event as a subject for poetry. Later poets with child audiences in mind have followed worlds of reality, fantasy, and nonsense, but have mainly avoided overt moralizing and didactics.

Silverstein's genius lies, of course, in finding a new way to present moralism, beguiling his child readers with a technique that establishes him as both an errant, mischievous, and inventive child as well as an understanding, trusted, and wise adult. One cannot find in his cautionary tales the hellfire and brimstone of Watts, the fear-ridden disasters of *Struwwelpeter*, the witty condescensions of Hilaire Belloc, or the happy-ever-after ending of Maurice Sendak's *Pierre*. Silverstein's tales are a new genre, narrated with seeming levity, but never shrinking from moral retribution.

If Sarah Sylvia Cynthia Stout refuses to empty the garbage,

she deserves the "awful fate" she meets, which Silverstein never divulges. If Jimmy Jet turns into a television set, it is just punishment for overwatching. Abigail dies because she is spoiled; Milford Dupree's mouth is glued together because he talks with "his mouth full of food"; "the long-haired boy," despite adult admonitions, insists on flying and is never seen again. Children recognize, to be sure, the unlikelihood of such possibilities, but they also recognize themselves guilty of disobedience, balking at chores, nagging, and poor manners. This is a subtle didacticism, narrated with humor, but it makes its point: those who defy authority, parental or otherwise, are in trouble.

> Listen to the MUSTN'TS, child,
> Listen to the DON'TS
> Listen to the SHOULDN'TS
> The IMPOSSIBLES, the WON'TS
> Listen to the NEVER HAVES
> Then listen close to me—
> Anything can happen, child,
> ANYTHING can be.

There is far more to Silverstein's moralism, however, than cautionary tales. In "Listen to the MUSTN'TS" lie his beliefs that children must not be expected to go it alone, that they need someone to guide them. But Silverstein knows that children abhor preaching, that they will defy those who would restrain them from "idleness and mischief." He understands just as well that to live only by dreary admonitions, to accept every danger sign and every warning, leads to apathy and dullness. He urges them, therefore, to look at the rules, the manners, the "Ations" (consideration, communication, cooperation) that keep the world together, that establish friendship and love, but also to learn to distinguish which of the "SHOULDN'TS" and "MUSTN'TS" can be attacked and ridiculed as he himself has done. Like Blake, Carroll, and Stevenson, he wishes children play, dreams, and pleasure. Like Lear he dares them to challenge the "theys" who would accept war, pollution, prejudice, and mammon. Like Watts he points out the lazy, greedy, and indolent.

But Silverstein's greatest contribution, indeed one of the most original yet made in the field of children's verse, is portrayed vividly on the cover of *A Light in the Attic*: the exhortation to children to not only look and see and listen to the world, but to turn on the light in *their* attic, to create for themselves, to *use their own imaginations!* In a world where adults recognize that children's imaginations are atrophying daily, that they no longer seem able to make their own pictures and images but depend on television and other sources to create for them, Silverstein figuratively pushes them out to the sidewalk's edge! Imagine, he says in dozens of verses, that a poem can be written from inside a lion or on the neck of a running giraffe. Pretend that your hands are cymbals, invent a light bulb that will plug into the sun, make an iron mask from a tin pail, polish stars, use an eel for a hula hoop, fly off in a shoe. No matter how wild, how inane, dare to dream and dare to do the impossible. It is not enough to be happy; indeed "The Land of Happy" where "everyone's happy all day" is a bore, as is the life of Mo, who has memorized the dictionary. Pity the plodders, Silverstein says, the "other folks" who have "never tried nothin' at all." But do not mistake materialism for creativity. Feel sorry for "ol' man Simon" who owns a garden of jewels but cannot find "One . . . real . . . peach" to eat. Consider that if the pot of gold is found, there is nothing more for which to search.

Silverstein wants children to

> Put something silly in the world
> That ain't been there before. . . .

to "play at hug o' war" instead of "tug o' war." He has made his magic in word and picture but advises that

> all the magic I have known
> I've had to make myself.

He will build them the bridge,

> But this bridge will only take you halfway there—
> The last few steps you'll have to take alone.

It is a new kind of morality that Silverstein calls for—one of creation and invention. Silverstein's concern with the need for imagination is often symbolized in verses about his head, a head that overflows with rain, blows away in a strange wind, says terrible things when stolen, and sprouts a "twisty and thorny and branchy and bare" tree that will change in Spring. In two unusual verses he offers the reader his head, broiled on a platter and, indeed, all of his body made into a "Me-Stew."

Do children recognize that Silverstein is exhorting them to this new moralism? Probably not. No more than they recognize his many metrically mangled lines, use of shoddy form, and occasional poor grammar. Shel Silverstein is not a poet of craftsmanship, but he is a magnificent poet of the spirit, and what he says in light verse and drawing to children is of such importance, such urgency that we must be grateful that over five million copies of these two books alone are being read. In a world that needs a generation of imaginative thinkers, may there be millions and millions more!

VALERIE WORTH (1933–   )
Valerie Worth's Treasures

There are few poets writing for children today whose metaphoric eye is keener than that of Valerie Worth. Her four books *Small Poems, More Small Poems, Still More Small Poems,* and *Small Poems Again,* published between 1972 and 1986, are testament to the excellence that poetry for the young offers. Hers is the gift not only of heightened consciousness but of an ability to make comparisons between objects that immediately awaken readers to new perspectives. A closed safety pin

> sleeps
> On its side
> Quietly,
> The silver
> Image
> Of some
> Small fish;

whereas

> Opened, it snaps
> Its tail out
> Like a thin

> Shrimp, and looks
> At the sharp
> Point with a
> Surprised eye.

What reader can ever again look at a safety pin as a mere utilitarian object?

While many others seek to entertain children with instant laughter, Worth invites children to observe the world about them, to value the commonplace articles that make up their everyday world—from clocks, hollyhocks, and chairs to creatures at the zoo. Like haiku, Worth's poems are written in the present tense, and are each of one thing keenly observed, inviting readers to complete the picture. Unlike haiku, they are not limited by subject matter or syllable pattern. Each word is carefully chosen, arranged in rhythms that emphasize the power of onomatopoeia. She writes of

> Hard leather heels,
> Their blocks carved
> Thick, like rocks,
> Clacked down
> Waxed wood stairs,

and of the

> pale soles
> Of sneakers. . . .

Worth's treasures do not lie in some distant, golden land but in the everyday world. She shows us earthworms who

> Glisten in the sun
> As fresh
> As new rubies

        Dug out of
        Deepest earth

Her

        . . . round jewels,
        Slithering gold

are marbles poured into their bag. A hose

        Can rain
        Chill diamond
        Chains
        Across the yard

or

        . . . hang
        A silk
        Rainbow
        Halo
        Over soft fog.

In the garbage she finds

        Hammered-gold
        Orange rind,

        Eggshell ivory,
        Garnet coffee-
        Grounds, pearl
        Wand of bared
        Chicken bone.

Riches to her are "satin sea lions," the "sleek velvets" on the back of a mosquito, and the lions' "plush-covered clay."

    Eschewing singsong meter and incessant end-rhyme, Worth brilliantly employs other aspects of the poet's craft.

Through personification she notes the "soft skull" and "frail ribs" of a mushroom, a lawnmower that

> Grinds its teeth
> Over the grass
> Spitting out a thick
> Green spray;
>
> Its head is too full
> Of iron and oil
> To know
> What it throws
> Away.

Telephone poles sweat "Black creosote," and coat hangers

> Clash and cling,
> And fling them-
> Selves to the
> Floor in an
> Inextricable tangle.

She invites children, through simile and metaphor, to notice asparagus

> Like a nest
> Of snakes
> Awakened, craning
> Long-necked
>
> Out of the
> Ground: to stand
> With sharp
> Scaly heads
>
> Alert, tasting
> The air,

Taking the sun,
Looking around.

The frog's

gold-circled eyes
Stare hard
Like bright metal rings.

Porch chairs

wait, arranged,
Strange and polite,

whereas field grass

Whistles, slides,

and

Tangles itself
With leaves . . .

Her rhythms mesh with subject.

This clock
Has stopped,
Some gear
Or spring
Gone wrong.

Fireworks follow their accustomed ascent:

First
A far thud,
Then the rocket
Climbs the air,
A dull red flare,

> To hang, a moment,
> Invisible, before
> Its shut black shell cracks. . . .

Alliteratively, she observes the beetle's

> lacquered
> Coffer of
> Curious
> Compartments

or how

> The slug
> Slides sly.

Rhyme is used judiciously, often internally or as slant rhyme. A masterful use of synesthesia occurs in

> The harsh gold
> Smell of lions.

Worth's pragmatism is evident in several lyrical forays. She believes that a sparrow

> Is as good a bird
> As anyone needs.

A magnet, she writes,

> Is sold for
> A toy . . .

and picks up pins but

> . . . later
> It lies about
> Getting its red

Paint chipped, being
Offered pins less
Often, until at
Last we leave it
Alone: . . .

This pragmatisim and a touch of quiet underlying humor is most evident in her fictional works, *Gypsy Gold* and *Curlicues*. Here she employs a simple yet elegant prose style. Here, as storyteller, she weaves into beautifully cadenced prose the same artful and judicious use of metaphor, simile, and personification that characterizes her poetry.

On Poetry

Mendacious Dwarfs
and Mountebanks

I'll tell you the truth, Father, though your heart bleed:
  To the Play I went,
With sixpence for a near seat, money's worth indeed,
  The best ever spent.

You forbade me, you threatened me, but here's the story
  Of my splendid night:
It was colour, drums, music, a tragic glory,
  Fear with delight.

Hamlet, Prince of Denmark, title of the tale:
  He of that name,
A tall glum fellow, velvet cloaked, with a shirt of mail,
  Two eyes like flame.

All the furies of Hell circled round that man,
  Maddening his heart,
There was old murder done before play began,
  Aye, the ghost took part.

There were grave-diggers delving, they brought up bones,
  And with rage and grief
All the players shouted in full, kingly tones,
  Grand, passing belief.

Ah, there were ladies there radiant as day,
  And changing scenes:
Fabulous words were tossed about like hay
  By kings and queens.

I puzzled on the sense of it in vain,
  Yet for pain I cried,
As one and all they faded, poisoned or slain,
  In great agony died.

Drive me out, Father, never to return,
  Though I am your son,
And penniless! But that glory for which I burn
  Shall be soon begun:

I shall wear great boots, shall strut and shout,
  Keep my locks curled;
The fame of my name shall go ringing about
  Over half the world.

What more remarkable proof do we need of that which
children take from poetry than Robert Graves suggests in
this poem, "The Forbidden Play"? His testament of the power
of apprehension over—indeed, in place of—comprehension is powerful and deserves further attention. A boy has
gone to see *Hamlet*, tells his father that he "puzzled on
the sense of it in vain," yet still cried for pain. What a
confirmation of James Stephens's belief in *The Crock of
Gold* that "What the heart knows today, the head will understand tomorrow." What an apt example of Robert
Frost's belief that poetry begins in delight and ends in
wisdom!

It is, Graves says, the way of the child to be dazzled by
color, drums, music, tragic glory, great boots, and fabulous

words tossed about like hay. But it is unnecessary to understand all that happens, to try to make sense of everything
at a certain age. What lives on one level, what *is* important,
is the recognition that within great literature all the symbols
are there to be mulled over, the delight and the pain, the
glory and the mystery. What lives above all is the hope,
dream, and wonder that possess the young.

Graves is concerned with children and their apprehension
in *The Penny Fiddle*. He is obsessed with the "fewness,
muchness, greatness of this endless only precious world
in which we live," and its effects on the imagination of
the child. Certainly these are concerns that have consumed
all of us who live much of our lives in the service of children
and books. We want our children to glean from literature
the fabulous words, the tragic glory; we want them to put
on great boots.

Does Graves call his poem "The Forbidden Play" with
tongue-in-cheek? *The Tragedy of Hamlet, Prince of Denmark*, for all its murder, ghost, grave-diggers, war, daggers,
poison, and Furies of Hell, would seem to most, today,
rather tame in comparison to *The Exorcist*, *Poltergeist*, and
The Evil, to mention but three films viewed by children in
movie theaters and on television. Can the spilling of blood—
the deaths of Ophelia, Polonius, Claudius, Gertrude, and
Hamlet himself—be measured against the devils living
within a possessed child, evil spirits living in houses and
in bedrock? *Hamlet*—forbidden? It is a curious idea to con-
template.

It is doubtful that anyone would disagree that *Hamlet* is
one of the masterpieces of literature. Its passages, its ideas
and words assail us in our everyday lives, and its symbols

offer us a variety of approaches as individuals and in our communication with and knowledge of others. Claudius and Gertrude inhabit our neighborhoods, Polonius offers us advice, Rosenkrantz and Guildenstern play with our children, Horatio and Laertes are the friends we telephone. And what of Hamlet? Does he not live in us and those we know, the man of high moral values, of intellect and wit, who recognizes the evil around him, who is desperately and profoundly aware that in times out of joint, matters must be set aright, but who—for some reason—cannot act wisely?

The tragedy of *Hamlet* is not the deaths and murders. The tragedy is that Hamlet *cannot* act until it is too late, and that Fortinbras, who *is* able to make decisions, will inherit his world, and his great boots. The tragedy is that Fortinbras is a lesser man than Hamlet, and *that* is the rage and grief, the pain that the child apprehends but does not comprehend. It is for us to understand and to foresee, for we are no longer children.

> Nobody who knows and loves real books is very satisfied with substitutes. . . . And yet, deleted, emasculated and cheaply decorated editions of well-known children's books, and new titles of commonplace spineless, poorly written books continue to flow in and out of reviewers' offices every year, leaving the reviewer sick to death of children's books in the mass. . . . Too many children's books are being published to-day and far too many cover jackets for books, both new and old, are being devised for quick sales rather than to fit the book or to please the child for whom the book is intended. . . . Promiscuous merchandizing of "juveniles" with small regard for authorship, illustration, or content has

flooded the market with substitutes for children's books in bright, meaningless cover jackets tagged with various ages of unknown and sadly neglected readers,

yet good books "are the best possible fortification against the vulgarity, the materialistic conceptions and cheap fancy which characterize many of the popular books for little children."

These observations may sound familiar. They were written in 1924 by Anne Carroll Moore, and yet they persist, in different words, today. Is it possible that generations later we have not been able to act, to make changes, to see the problems and correct them? Is there reason to hope that we may do so now?

I like to think so. And in the field of poetry I am, for the most part, heartened by the persistence of excellence, an excellence that did not exist in 1924. The staples of my own childhood reading in poetry are still about—Robert Louis Stevenson, William Blake, Edward Lear, Lewis Carroll, Dorothy Aldis, Christina Rossetti, A. A. Milne, Rachel Field— but consigned to the forgotten are versifiers whose names have, for the most part, lost their luster. The rhyming haiku of *Little Pictures of Japan* has been replaced by a purer form. There are more than *100 Best Poems for Boys and Girls*. Mother Goose is alive and Tennyson still speaks with a sure voice. Longfellow, Eugene Field, and James Whitcomb Riley are only resurrected by the sentimentalists. New voices, ever appearing, have spoken with surer knowledge of children, of a reality that moves beyond lamplighters and English chauvinism, and nonsense that leaves the Sugar Plum and the Amfalula Tree in the shade to die.

Yet there are some signs that we stand in danger of returning to times past, to the images that populate a world not in tune with our own. Such images would negate the spectrum of a broader, more tolerant world—a world that recognizes the contributions of all races and all peoples. In addition, insidiously creeping into poetry is that same malaise that has pervaded the so-called poetry children write—the image of the autonomous imagination, the nightmare of the child with no hope or help from adults, the fruitless wish, the lie, the surrealistic world for which there is no redeeming symbolism. Sometimes this tendency is overlooked. Poetry itself scares off many, and what would be questioned in other literary forms is not even recognized when clothed in rollicking verse, nonsense, or brightly colored illustrations.

The very word "poetry" often becomes a catchall for anything that is written in a certain pattern of lines. While anyone who seeks to define poetry is doomed to failure, it is possible to distinguish poetry from second-rate verse. Both use the same tools. Anyone can scatter words like hay, rearrange prose to resemble a poem. Anyone who has half an ear for rhyme and a sense of metrics can toss off a passable verse. The distinction occurs not in the way the words are placed, but in the tone. Poets show respect for the child by revealing the child in themselves, by remembering experiences and emotions true to their own lives. Versifiers, on the contrary, are dulled to the feelings of childhood and condescendingly reshape their own faulty memories to a pattern of what childhood should be. Poor verse displays a lack of understanding of how a child looks at the world; what is written *tells* rather than *shows*. Concepts substitute for good imagery. Versifiers forget that children do not deal in concepts—pride, love, anger, pity. Very few do not admit apprehension, insisting on sense and reason. Such poor verse often attempts to clothe an adult's idea of wisdom in false trappings of delight. A strong desire to indoctrinate youth with values, to instruct, a propensity to catalog, to present encylopedic information, are the telltale signs of dull, didactic verse. Every stanza, rhymed or un-rhymed, is a lesson that must be presented and hammered in. Examples of such verse can be seen in a widely circulated recent anthology where the adult wishes to show the joy of words. One verse says:

> Words are wonderful.
> Words are weird:
>> wanton, wicked,
>> writhing, witless,
>> wrathful, winsome,
>> whooping, whispering,
>> woebegone, withering,
>> warping, weakening,
>> wanting, wresting,
>> worrisome, wincing,
>> wishful, winning.
> Words are weird.
> Words are wonderful.

Given a long catalog of words that begin with *W* and *told* how wonderful and weird words are, most children, needless to say, will forever shun words. Equally distressing is the piece that presumes the child will be beguiled by the false lyrical voice, the feigned friendship.

> I hope that I shall never be
> Devoid of curiosity

About the meaning of a word
Which I have either seen or heard.

I hope when of a word I'm wary
I'll always seek a dictionary,
And learn to use it as a friend
For help and counsel without end.

Other verses that begin

I like stand-up words.
        straight still
I like sit-down words.
        slide spill
I like scary words.
        Whooo's there?

are equally put-offs. Indeed, one cannot imagine the child
who would do much besides fidget and yawn when asked:

Words are the oddest things
        Haven't you found?
Sometimes they don't look a
        Bit like they sound.

There are "to," "too," and "two."
        Watch which you're using!
If you're not a good speller, it's
        Very confusing.

Sometimes one word can mean
        Different things;
We draw with straight "rulers"
        Or else it means "kings."

When you recite "bow,"
        But shoot with a "bow."

> Words are the oddest things!
> Don't you think so?

Occasionally the versifier strives for metaphor and comes up with a long verse that begins:

> Words are little singing sounds
> for saying over and over.
> They run in little bootstep tracks
> on pages, cover to cover,
> They make us bridges and trees and pigs
> and a house for a little red hen.
> They let us see things all over the world
> without even pictures of them.

To compare any of these to poetry is to recognize how poets avoid ordered lists, false goodness, and coy references to "stand-up" or "sit-down" words as well as foolish questions. There is no fuzzy "bootstep track," no "house for a little red hen," in David McCord's "Take Sky."

> Now think of words. Take *Sky*
> And ask yourself just why—
> Like sun, moon, star, and cloud—
> It sounds so well out loud,
> And pleases so the sight
> When printed black on white.
> Take syllable and thimble:
> The sound of *them* is nimble.
> Take bucket, spring, and dip
> Cold water to your lip.
> Take balsam, fir, and pine:
> Your woodland smell and mine.
> Take kindle, blaze, and flicker—
> What lights the hearth fire quicker?

Three words we fear but form:
Gale, twister, thunderstorm;
Others that simply shake
Are tremble, temblor, quake.
But granite, stone, and rock:
Too solid, they, to shock.
Put honey, bee, and flower
With sunny, shade, and shower;
Put *wild* with bird and wing,
Put *bird* with song and sing.
Aren't paddle, trail, and camp
The cabin and the lamp?
Now look at words of rest—
Sleep, quiet, calm, and blest;

At words we learn in youth—
Grace, skill, ambition, truth;
At words of lifelong need—
Grit, courage, strength, and deed;
Deep-rooted words that say
Love, hope, dream, yearn, and pray;
Light-hearted words—girl, boy,
Live, laugh, play, share, enjoy.
October, April, June—
Come late and gone too soon.
Remember, words are life:
Child, husband, mother, wife;
Remember, and I'm done:
Words taken one by one

Are poems as they stand—
Shore, beacon, harbor, land;
Brook, river, mountain, vale,

Crow, rabbit, otter, quail;
Faith, freedom, water, snow,
Wind, weather, flood, and floe.
Like light across the lawn
Are morning, sea, and dawn;
Words of the green earth growing—
Seed, soil, and farmer sowing.
Like wind upon the mouth
Sad, summer, rain, and south.
Amen. Put not asunder
Man's *first* word: wonder . . . wonder . . .

Poor verse can be distinguished from real poetry in these brief examples, perhaps more than in any other way, through the knowledge that verse presupposes the child to be so innocent as to have only happy thoughts open to "little singing sounds" and completely without the darker side of life. The versifier, in addition to wishing to cram encyclopedic knowledge, Happy Mr. Sun, and Beneficient Dame Nature down children's throats, is someone who has forgotten what childhood is really like, who has a magic formula for imparting not only information, but information that is of a happy nature. Forefathers have "courage true," covered wagons are faithful, soldiers are loyal; the goldenrod, for the two-hundredth time, is yellow, and the leaves are aflutter or forever turning brown; fires ablaze, Columbus is wise, there is magic in the name of October, and winter brings a wealth of "jolly things." But the worst of it is that beyond high-sounding concepts and trite and stereotyped views, beyond singsong verse and pedestrian rhyme, the poor versifier admits to no knowledge of the darker side of human nature, that which is as much a part of the child as the laughter and merry and happy thoughts. The child cannot, in short, cry for pain because the versifier's distorted memory of childhood will not allow it. *Hamlet* is forbidden; tragic glory simply does *not* exist.

This is not to condone the preoccupation with the darker side of the unconscious, the insistence that children be confronted with nightmare and monsters that lurk outside the school, the ugliness of human nature, the absent or ineffective adult, the mean and nasty child or animal whose exploits are glorified and whose aberrant nature prevails, all disguised in happy anapestic rhythms, pleasing rhyme, and decorated with illustrations that depict children with faces that resemble distorted plastic masks and pinched Silly Putty. For these offshoots of the second-rate young-adult novel have begun to creep into verse for younger children: These are not the symbols of a *Hamlet*, but the glorification of the bizarre, the pseudosurrealistic stance, the ersatz nonsense that has pervaded the writing of those who deal in autonomous images instead of rich symbolism. "What matters," George Steiner has written, "is truth and splendor of human experience in the light of conflict," but in all this there is no chance for truth or splendor. Here the ghost does not come to ask for revenge but to inflict it; there is no Marcellus; no Laertes appears to whom to turn.

There is, of course, a place for image in the verse we share with children. Not all that is given in the beginning can be rich in symbolism. There need be only a gradual progression from verse to poetry, but too often no distinction is made, and children are forever left with an adequate expression for delight but no knowledge of how to express the wonder or seek answers for their pain. Their bubbling spirits, their desire for story, their release in coenesthesia—that combination of mental and physical response to poetry—can be easily gratified by an image that instantly engages.

> Now, I'm not the one
> To say No to a bun,
> And I always can manage some jelly;
> If somebody gurgles,
> "Please eat my hamburgles,"
> I try to make room in my belly.
> I seem, if they scream,
> Not to gag on ice-cream;
> And with fudge I can choke down my fright;
> But none is enticing
> Or even worth slicing,
> Compared with Garbage Delight.

> > With a nip and a nibble
> > A drip and a dribble
> > A dollop, a walloping bite:
> > If you want to see grins
> > All the way to my shins,
> > Then give me some Garbage Delight!

> I'm handy with candy.
> I star with a bar.
> And I'm known for my butterscotch burp;
> I can stare in the eyes
> Of a Toffee Surprise
> And polish it off with one slurp.

My lick is the longest,
My chomp is the champ
And everyone envies my bite;
But my talents were wasted
Until I had tasted
The wonders of Garbage Delight.
    With a nip and a nibble
    A drip and a dribble
    A dollop, a walloping bite:
    If you want to see grins
    All the way to my shins
    Then give me some Garbage Delight,
        Right now!
    Please pass me the Garbage Delight

The thought that eating garbage is preferable to fudge and hamburgers and ice cream is, of course, appealing to the child who learns through nonsense what sense is. In "Garbage Delight" Dennis Lee has pulled out the stops: mixed up words, offered shock value with words such as "belly" and "burp," employed alliteration and internal and end rhyme. His clever craftsmanship has given the child an image—someone preferring garbage to food—in upbeat anapestic rhythm.

On the same subject, garbage, here is another voice using the concept as a takeoff point for a story, a cautionary verse, a verse that initiates us into the catalog poem, which lists in detail the contents of garbage cans:

Sarah Cynthia Sylvia Stout
Would not take the garbage out!
She'd scour the pots and scrape the pans,
Candy the yams and spice the hams,

And though her daddy would scream and shout,
She simply would not take the garbage out.
And so it piled up to the ceilings:
Coffee grounds, potato peelings,
Brown bananas, rotten peas,
Chunks of sour cottage cheese.
It filled the can, it covered the floor,
It cracked the window and blocked the door
With bacon rinds and chicken bones,
Drippy ends of ice cream cones,
Prune pits, peach pits, orange peel,
Gloppy glumps of cold oatmeal,
Pizza crusts and withered greens,
Soggy beans and tangerines,
Crusts of black burned buttered toast,
Bristly bits of beefy roasts . . .
The garbage rolled on down the hall,
It raised the roof, it broke the wall . . .
Greasy napkins, cookie crumbs,
Globs of gooey bubble gum
Cellophane from green baloney,
Rubbery blubbery macaroni,
Peanut butter, caked and dry,
Curdled milk and crusts of pie,
Moldy melons, dried-up mustard,
Eggshells mixed with lemon custard,
Cold french fries and rancid meat,
Yellow lumps of Cream of Wheat.
At last the garbage reached so high
That finally it touched the sky.
And all the neighbors moved away,
And none of her friends would come to play.
And finally Sarah Cynthia Stout said,

"OK, I'll take the garbage out!"
But then, of course, it was too late . . .
The garbage reached across the state,
From New York to the Golden Gate.
And there, in the garbage she did hate,
Poor Sarah met an awful fate,
That I cannot right now relate
Because the hour is much too late.
But children, remember Sarah Stout
And always take the garbage out!

Here is a masterpiece of hyperbole that not only offers a listing of all the kinds of garbage children might recognize, but allows an opportunity to hear a story whose end can be further supplied by the child's imagination. Shel Silverstein offers more here than pure nonsense, for nonsense does not admit the possibilities of change nor even concern for what is happening. And Silverstein is a moralist who hovers between nonsense and reality.

But nonsense, whether pure or adulterated, *does* present the image, and a more palatable one than is found in the realists. Early childhood is the time to sort out, to find comparisons, to relate to the self. Dorothy Aldis in "Like Me" begins with

A garbage man is a garbage man
Who rattles and bangs the garbage can.

Like me.

Beyond the reality, the understanding of what a garbage man does and how he may be similar or different, there may be the child who sees in the garbage man a certain adventure.

Here comes Varge
Picking up the garbage cans!
Here comes Varge
In his rattle-rattle truck!
The Monday-morning garbage man!
Varge is coming in his great red truck!

I wish that I were Varge's boy
And helped him with his garbage cans,
I wish that I were Varge's boy
And rode a garbage truck.
Then Varge and I would drive around
All over town, all over town,
Then Varge and I would pal around
And drive the garbage truck!

Patricia Hubbell's "Varge" accepts the reality of garbage
and the means by which it is hauled away. Here is no
nonsense, but a jumping-off place for adventure and friendship. In unrhymed verse that uses repetition to engender
the excitement the child feels, the image of the rattling
truck and the man who drives it is a step beyond the comparison and sorting out that Aldis relays, the tiniest spark of
the dream of glory.

In Robert Froman's "Greedy" the garbage truck becomes
an image couched in metaphoric terms. Most children
can immediately relate to this image, but it is one that has
been done over and over again; the machine that
feeds on stones; the animal, the door of the house that
gobbles and swallows whatever is put into its mouth. The
greedy mouth is little more than stereotype. "Greedy" is a
realistic picture of garbage with the animism young children
delight in.

Big pile

of

Here comes the garbage truck.

GOBBBLLLLLE.

Beyond the early years, young people may respond to the work of James Schevill, whose poem "What Are the Most Unusual Things You Find in Garbage Cans?" appears in *Some Haystacks Don't Even Have Any Needle*. Here Schevill assumes the persona of ten trashmen who explain what they find in garbage cans. Burristrezzi begins:

After a wedding or baby shower
I find
lots of gifts in the garbage.
What you don't like, you throw away,
I guess.
Sell it, you're a cheapskate,
Give it, you feel guilty,
So you chuck it in the garbage.

Benson says:

In the trash
behind the old Hall of Justice
once
I found a wooden leg.

Hamilton tells us:

Old books
you never saw
so many
god damn
old books
with weird titles
like
"Rebecca of Sunnybrook Farm"

And the painter says:

Cash
wristwatches
and a gold
wedding ring

In free, unrhymed verse the reader learns what these and the six other men find. Images of an old espresso machine, baby cribs, helmets, girly pictures, a lot of picture frames, a houseful of radios complete the picture. Listening to the poem might then inform us that garbage cans are filled with a myriad of things and show the men's reactions. But the total effect, again, remains one of a catalog of images. It is true that Schevill has spoken of the unusual things—not the garbage that Sarah Stout refuses to empty, the stuff that Dennis Lee's child passes up, or the contents of Robert Froman's garbage cans.

"Image," of course, is the magic word. Give us images, poets say, and therein lies poetry. Give us images in words. But are words enough? Do we not need, in fact, more, and does the child not deserve more than such listings? Nonsense, to be sure, is delightful—and the sorting out of peoples' tasks and how they compare to the individual is part of growing and self-identification. The wish to be a garbageman can certainly be a part of childhood.

But there must be more; there must be real poetry that, through careful ordering and selection, turns image—in this case, garbage—into symbol. Poetry is not merely words in lists, nor an arrangement that brings to mind a picture. The picture, like the haiku, must be just a beginning—and it should lead on to the wonder, the possibilities for growth and for relating to the unknown.

The subject is still garbage; the poem is "The City Dump."

> City asleep
> City asleep
> Papers fly at the garbage heap.
> Refuse dumped and
> The sea gulls reap
> Grapefruit rinds

And coffee grinds
And apple peels.
The sea gull reels and
The field mouse steals
In for a bite
At the end of night
Of crusts and crumbs
And pits of plums.
The white eggshells
And the green-blue smells
And the gray gull's cry
And the red dawn sky . . .
City asleep
City asleep
A carnival
On the garbage heap.

What we have here is more than a listing of items to be found in the garbage. Felice Holman has judiciously selected grapefruit rinds and coffee grounds, apple peels, pits of plums, white eggshells, and papers; she has made a carnival where sea gulls and field mice come; she has painted a further picture of a city asleep. In doing so she has given rein to the creative imagination of the listener. What magic is performed, elsewhere, as we are asleep, what other life goes on, what is the end of the garbage we toss away by day? She has set young minds stretching beyond image into symbol.

The art of the poet is to order, to select, and to add to that selection even more, to transform through metaphor the old garbage into something new. Even children must first make sense of what is and what is not, and transform their own lives. The art of the poet is to allow the reader to find something new—something never seen before, something never thought of before—and in doing so make possible the very idea of change.

> The stained,
> Sour-scented
> Bucket tips out
> Hammered gold
> Orange rind,
>
> Eggshell ivory,
> Garnet coffee-
> Grounds, pearl
> Wand of bared
> Chicken bone:
>
> Worked back soon
> To still more
> Curious jewelry
> Of chemical
> And molecule.

The sour-scented bucket, the orange rind, coffee grounds, eggshells, and chicken bones are still there, part of reality, in this poem. They are the poet's judicious selection. But what Valerie Worth has done beyond reality is to change these bits of garbage into jewelry of hammered gold, of ivory, of garnet and pearl wand. The poet sees in the ordinary the extraordinary, the metamorphosis that can be made through observation and imagination. Poetry opens up possibilities—suggests ways of looking in which we can create something new, different worlds for ourselves. This is no longer image, but symbol!

It is a long way from the nonsense of "Garbage Delight" to the jewels of Valerie Worth. In between there are verses and rhythms and various levels appealing to children. And yes, we should laugh at the nonsense and accept the real, recognizing that each has its place, whether for humor or dream or glory or friendship or wonder. But if we champion only comprehension, only understanding, we will cling to the listings.

What I am suggesting is not that we ignore the image—indeed it is, whether humorous or serious, necessary—but that we not allow ourselves to be content with image, with laughter alone. Delight is necessary in our lives, but it does not answer all of our needs, nor does it answer those of children. They know fear and pain as deeply as we and come to learn that mere autonomous wish or dream does not make the pain any easier to bear. It is important that we give children nonsense, for, as Kornei Chukovsky tells us, it is one way of attaining self-worth. But to give children *only* nonsense, to pretend that poetry is sugar-coated rhythm and rhyme and image, is to rob them of the ability to deal with more serious aspects of life that they will surely meet, in ways we do not even suspect.

For who can prophesy what they will encounter and how they will solve the unforeseen problems of times to come? To offer children symbol, to offer metaphor, is to ensure that they will not have to face the specters of fear and pain without the knowledge that change is possible, that each can react in individual ways and act to make that change. Just as the happy rhythms, the delightful images that light verse and nonsense afford offer a sense of self-worth, a knowledge of what is and what is not, symbol offers the opportunity to respond beyond stereotype, beyond despair, with new insights and meaningful action. Symbol helps us learn that change is possible, that action is possible, and that each of us has the creativity to effect that change and action in a unique way.

"Every story we tell a child is a whole set of blueprints for dealing with himself and for dealing with his own imagination," Ted Hughes writes in "Myth and Imagination." To Hughes, the great works of imaginative literature are "hospitals where we heal, where our imaginations are healed. . . ." But when they are less than the great, when they are evil, they can be "battlefields where we get injured." It is important that children have the literature to help strengthen them so that they can cope with the evils. But if we give them the frightening image of a single poet's unconscious; if we offer them no help and tell them they must go it alone; if we portray adults as weak and defenseless; if we abolish the kind helpmeet of the folk and fairy tale, we can expect no better than crippled, hobbled, and dark individuals to inherit our world.

It is the same for poetry, perhaps even more so. For poetry is absorbed, through its music and rhythms, into our blood; its lines, its symbols return to us throughout life. And if we do not offer the best in poetry, that most succinct form of literature, if we give only didactic exhortations, easy-to-understand verse, or even confine reading to the fleeting image, we cheat ourselves and our children of those symbols that sustain and strengthen us when times are out of joint.

Too often, as George Steiner points out, we have become

prey to "a sort of nervous exhaustion, of entropy, in the inward resources of Western Culture. We seem to be governed by more or less mendacious dwarfs and mountebanks. Our responses to crises display a certain somnambular automatism. Our arts and letters are, arguably, those of epigones."

These are depressing words—difficult words—but because we deal with children does not mean that we, like children, show lack of reason in understanding them and fall prey to the lying dwarfs and storytelling charlatans who offer us a bag of rhythmic pills and word tricks. If we let undistinguished imitators take over, if we allow ourselves to be led at every turn by amateur reviewers rather than seasoned critics, by the rawness of personal opinion or by an advertising campaign, we are indeed abdicating our responsibility.

There are many kinds of responsibility. That of the poet's obligation began with Isaac Watts in the seventeenth century. Dr. Watts wisely advocated the use of rhyme as an aid to remembrance but, not so enticingly, wished to impart virtue through use of didacticism, by stressing studiousness, duty to work, and purpose in all things. The sluggard spends his time eating and dreaming, thus allowing Satan and false gods to work their wiles. Bible study, "redeeming love and renewing grace," are exemplified, in this instance, by the busy bee.

> How doth the little busy bee
>   Improve each shining hour,
> And gather honey all the day
>   From every opening flower.

How skillfully she builds her cell!
How neatly spreads the wax!
And labours hard to store it well
With the sweet food she makes.

In works of labour or of skill,
I would be busy too;
For Satan finds some mischief still
For idle hands to do.

In books, or work, or healthful play,
Let my first years be passed,
That I may give for everyday
Some good account at last.

Against Watts and his followers, William Blake responded with fervor. It is the priests who wind the briars and thorns in the sluggard's garden; the false nurse of *Songs of Experience* who does not allow the children to play a bit longer; the unfeeling adult who rails against the pleasures of food and the importance of dreams. Lewis Carroll's attack was no less vehement.

How doth the little crocodile
Improve his shining tail
And pour the waters of the Nile
On every golden scale!

How cheerfully he seems to grin,
How neatly spreads his claws,
And welcomes little fishes in
With gently smiling jaws!

Dr. Watts is the crocodile who seeks to improve through his "golden scales"—his hymns—all the time feigning a false cheerfulness that destroys the right of children to real play, dreams, and pleasures. Carroll fought mischief by making it against Southey, Watts, and all others who would deny children their few years of innocent joy.

However we may view the attitudes of these pioneers toward children and poetry, they have survived to this day because the adherence to the idea of nature as model is rich in symbolism and highly moral in tone. The responsibility of the poets is to strengthen through their work the fibers of a child's life, either through a serious observation of the world, or to the inner need for response through imagination and nonsense. The world of reality and play has been exemplified in Robert Louis Stevenson, the world of nonsense and imagination in Edward Lear. Walter de la Mare wisely recognized that both are necessary, and this tradition lives through the work of most contemporary children's poets who present their views of the world, offering serious searches into the emotions and feelings of a child through meaningful symbol or through humor.

Similarly, the anthologist has always carried a responsibility to the young. The knowledge of what constitutes a good anthology begins with an understanding of what the word actually means, for it is often misused today by even the most informed. An anthology is not the work of *one* poet but a gathering of various authors—and in the Greek, a gathering of flowers. The milestone anthologies—Palgrave's *Golden Treasury*, de la Mare's *Come Hither*, Annis Duff and Gladys Adshead's *An Inheritance of Poetry*, and Herbert Read's *This Way Delight*—in their time collected flowers, with careful attention to the blending of images of levity and poetry of symbolism; flowers picked from many centuries and times with universal appeal. Many anthologists have continued this tradition during the past few decades and have offered excellence of subject and format. Yet amidst all this wealth, we are still prey to those who offer poor verse disguised as poetry, pedestrian words and images that ask children to walk among weeds. What strikes me as most curious is that in all other fields of children's literature—biography, nonfiction, novel and fantasy, picture books—there is vociferous response and debate to values portrayed. Yet all critical judgment seems to vanish when a book of poetry or an anthology appears. It is as though the very word "poetry" evokes feelings of the thing we ought to like and ought to have.

Many readers are apt, as A. E. Housman points out in *The Name and Nature of Poetry*, to admire poetry for the wrong reasons—and what is often accepted holus-bolus is not the selection but the packaging. Many readers judge an anthology by the illustrations, forgetting that good poetry makes its own pictures. Others become enchanted by the dust jacket, the name of the illustrator, the layout or the size of the book. Too many neglect to look in the index to discover what the anthologist has retained of the meaningful past and what has been added for the contemporary child. Too many respond to muted pastels and colorful page spreads that confirm "All's right with the world" if well-dressed, well-fed, innocent children peer at the happy bounties of nature, flowers and grass with a stereotyped smiling sun beaming from the right-hand corner of the page, while others accept as being modern and very much up-to-date anthologies that employ flashy photography, whether or not that photography suits the mood or words.

Few bother to investigate if an anthology is but a gathering of old public domain staples, chosen by an illustrator as a display for art. Many fail to notice the imbalance when a pseudoanthologist brings out a book as a showcase for his own work. And far too many overlook the fact that an anthology may include the work of a few well-known poets for window dressing, but that the bulk of the book is padded with second-rate verse, versifiers and weeds, a series of quick images reminiscent of the flashing images on television, quick laughs that are just as instantly forgotten.

The responsibility of those who buy books of individual poetry and anthologies, who share these books with children, is partially the ability to discriminate between poor verse and good light verse; to present image as a beginning, as delight, but to encourage children to move beyond to sustaining symbol. It is also to be aware that the forms of poetry often disguise meanings and that, beguiled by rhythm and rhyme, the choice is made to plunge the young into menacing images—and sometimes private symbols—that numb children, that threaten to leave them on a dismal battlefield. The craze for the urban, pseudosurrealistic view of the world that has held sway for almost a generation, that has created its own pop culture symbols and routed the traditional, has worked its wiles and worked them well. They have forgotten that, as William Carlos Williams believed, the poet's dream is not the individual nightmare, but a dream of vision, of possibility for a better world. Too many have begun to believe that the autonomous imagination and the aberrant is the only guide, that the darker side of the unconscious is where children must reside forever. The one who knows better stands ready to help where the sidewalk ends and leaves a light in the attic.

We cannot pretend that the Furies of Hell do not touch our children. What we can do is to offer fabulous words, recognizing that a foul murder takes place again and again when we do not act, when we do not stand up to those whose false mouthings urge us to keep still and face the fears alone. We have the fine poets, the dedicated anthologists, and the responsible editors and publishers to help. We *can* act before another generation has grown. The choice is ours.

> I am the only ME I AM
> who qualifies as me;
> no ME I AM has been before,
> and none will ever be.
>
> No other ME I AM can feel
> the feelings I've within;
> no other ME I AM can fit
> precisely in my skin.
>
> There is no other ME I AM
> who thinks the thoughts I do;
> the world contains one ME I AM,
> there is no room for two.
>
> I am the only ME I AM
> this earth shall ever see;
> that ME I AM *I* always am
> is no one else but ME!

Or:

> In the heel of my thumb
> are whorls, whirls, wheels

in a unique design:
mine alone.
What a treasure to own!
My own flesh, my own feelings.
No other, however grand or base,
can even contain the same.
My signature,
thumbing the pages of my time.
My universe key,
my singularity.
Impress, implant,
I am myself,
of all my atom parts I am the sum.
And out of my blood and my brain
I make my own interior weather,
my own sun and rain.
Imprint my mark upon the world,
whatever I shall become.

The choice is yours.

Imagination:
The Forms of
Things Unknown

hist   whist
little ghostthings
tip-toe
twinkle-toe

little twitchy
witches and tingling
goblins
hob-a-nob   hob-a-nob

little hoppy happy
toad in tweeds
tweeds
little itchy mousies

with scuttling
eyes   rustle and run   and
hidehidehide
whisk

whisk   look out for the old woman
with the wart on her nose
what she'll do to yer
nobody knows

for she knows the devil   ooch
the devil   ouch
the devil
ach   the great

green
dancing

devil
devil

devil
devil

           wheeEEE

I watch their faces. At first they think they haven't heard me correctly, that I am speaking too softly, so they quiet down. They appear not to understand the first few lines, but the words "tip-toe" and "twinkle-toe" arrest them; then "twitchy witches and tingling goblins." They like the alliteration of "hoppy happy toad in tweeds" and "rustle and run." They delight in being frightened. There is always embarrassment in a few boys at the back who haven't really been paying attention. It isn't good to show you like poetry all that much, anyhow. They pretend they didn't jump, that they weren't scared. By the time the devil comes along they are prepared to be surprised again, poised to jump at the word "wheeEEE." I go on to something else.

     'Twas brillig, and the slithy toves
       Did gyre and gimble in the wabe:
    All mimsy were the borogoves,
       And the mome raths outgrabe.

     "Beware the Jabberwock, my son!
       The jaws that bite, the claws that catch!

Beware the Jubjub bird, and shun
   The frumious Bandersnatch!"

He took his vorpal sword in hand:
   Long time the manxome foe he sought—
So rested he by the Tumtum tree,
   And stood awhile in thought.

And, as in uffish thought he stood,
   The Jabberwock, with eyes of flame,
Came whiffling through the tulgey wood,
   And burbled as it came!

One, two! One, two! And through and through
   The vorpal blade went snicker-snack!
He left it dead, and with its head
   He went galumphing back.

"And hast thou slain the Jabberwock?
   Come to my arms, my beamish boy!
O frabjous day! Callooh! Callay!"
   He chortled in his joy.

'Twas brillig, and the slithy toves
   Did gyre and gimble in the wabe:
All mimsy were the borogoves,
   And the mome raths outgrabe.

There was a time five years ago—ten years, fifteen—when a burst of recognition would greet "Jabberwocky." Some would mouth the words; some would wield imaginary swords or make grimaces at the mention of the Bandersnatch. It was a time for laughter, for fun. Everyone wanted to be slithy toves, the boy, the Jubjub bird, the Tumtum tree. They knew, instinctively, just how a mimsy borogove would behave.

But things have been very different lately, not just in California, where I first chalked it up to false sophistication, lack of meaningful contact with good literature, or ignorance of poetry in general. It happened in Dallas and in Wisconsin, cutting across all grade levels, all socioeconomic lines. Not that the students are deprived or overindulged or that teachers don't care. It's simply that students can't seem to make connections with words not explained; they are unaccustomed to the idea of intuitive response, unable to make the leap from sound to action, unwilling to take any chances at spontaneity. I do like to explain the meaning of the portmanteau words "frabjous," "frumious," and we usually end up learning the line " 'O frabjous day! Callooh! Callay!' " to be screamed out at moments when we've overcome a hurdle, like a difficult test. I seldom leave "Jabberwocky" without letting them know it's the most famous nonsense poem in the English language, that this is a bit of information they may wish to impart to their astounded mothers, and that they weren't supposed to understand the meaning of every word.

Understanding, comprehension, is *not* why we enjoy poetry; apprehension is.

A lot of seriously worrisome things have happened to Theodore Roethke's "Dinky."

> O what's the weather in a Beard?
> It's windy there, and rather weird,
> And when you think the sky has cleared
> 　—Why, there is Dirty Dinky.
>
> Suppose you walk out in a Storm,
> With nothing on to keep you warm,

And then step barefoot on a Worm
   —Of course, it's Dirty Dinky.

As I was crossing a hot hot Plain,
I saw a sight that caused me pain,
You asked me before, I'll tell you again:
   —It *looked* like Dirty Dinky.

Last night you lay a-sleeping? No!
The room was thirty-five below;
The sheets and blankets turned to snow.
   —He'd got in: Dirty Dinky.

You'd better watch the things you do.
You'd better watch the things you do.
You're part of him; he's part of you
   —*You* may be Dirty Dinky.

At Beverly Vista School, where I taught for many years,
all of the fifth-grade classes knew Dinky intimately five years
ago. I suspect that each of those one hundred thirty boys
and girls had a very personal, private Dinky. To some he
was small, even infinitesimal; to others, hulking, huge—
like a specter. He was brown, green, purple; his hair was
messy, or he had no hair and looked opaque. At one time
he even resembled the shark from *Jaws*. He stole lunches,
made it rain, emptied lockers, lost coats, left candy wrappers
under the bed, fouled up a proposed field trip with hail.
He was responsible for everything that went wrong.

Some months ago in Irvine I shared "Dinky." Almost
no one in six different classes, grades five through eight,
could tell me anything about him—his size, shape, color,
where he lived, or what he did. They just sat and looked
at me. The same thing happened in several schools in Dallas.

I keep telling myself that it isn't my lack of communication or ability to say the poem anymore, because I will always find one or two children in the room who smile knowingly at me. They catch the humor; they know the secret. But for every one of these children there used to be an entire classroom. I know, of course, they would all understand "Mr. Nobody."

> I know a funny little man,
>   As quiet as a mouse,
> Who does the mischief that is done
>   In everybody's house!
> There's no one ever sees his face,
>   And yet we all agree
> That every plate we break was cracked
>   By Mr. Nobody.
>
> 'Tis he who always tears our books,
>   Who leaves the door ajar,
> He pulls the buttons from our shirts,
>   And scatters pins afar;
> That squeaking door will always squeak,
>   For, prithee, don't you see,
> We leave the oiling to be done,
>   By Mr. Nobody. . . .

But *I* don't like Mr. Nobody because his anonymous creator has *told* me *who* he is and *where* he is and *what* he does—to the letter. There is no room left for my imagination. He is no match for Dinky, who can roam freely outside and in, who will adjust himself to the eyes of the beholder— and even, on occasion, be within the beholder. Mr. Nobody is too pat, too cutesy, too predictable, too much a caricature of himself. "Mr. Nobody" is, in short, reproductive imagination—mental pictures of what *has* been, of what *is* known. "Dinky," on the other hand, invites productive and creative imagination, projecting mental pictures, possibilities never before experienced.

> And as imagination bodies forth
> The forms of things unknown, the poet's pen
> Turns them to shapes, and gives to airy nothing
> A local habitation and a name.
> Such tricks hath strong imagination
> That, if it would but apprehend some joy,
> It comprehends some bringer of that joy;
> Or in the night, imagining some fear,
> How easy is a bush supposed a bear!

It isn't easy anymore to suppose a bush a bear, to give to airy nothing a name or a place. It occurs to me that *A Midsummer Night's Dream* has turned, of late, into a *Nightmare*, and the frenzy with which the poet's eye rolls is not so fine, after all. Apathy has replaced imagination in a series of activities that attend the child in school and at home. Atrophy has set in at many levels. How and why this has happened is open to speculation, even to disagreement; we are all aware of some of the causes. We cannot feel total responsibility for what has occurred; and yet, it seems to me that it is time to retrace our steps—find out where we are and where the children are—and try to restore whatever of the creative imagination we can. Where do we start?

Perhaps we can begin with a reexamination of what we believe to be reproductive imagination, passive imagination, and creative imagination, all of which can be detected quite easily in poetry and verse. Here is the reproductive, a series of mental pictures or images recalled:

> There was a little turtle.
> He lived in a box.
> He swam in a puddle.
> He climbed on the rocks.
>
> He snapped at a mosquito.
> He snapped at a flea.
> He snapped at a minnow.
> And he snapped at me.
>
> He caught the mosquito.
> He caught the flea.
> He caught the minnow.
> But he didn't catch me.

A pleasant verse by Vachel Lindsay, certainly—one worthy of engaging the young child in happy memory. But remembering how a turtle would behave is *not* creating, *not* being in touch with fancy.

> "Far enough down is China," somebody said.
> "Dig deep enough and you might see the sky
> As clear as at the bottom of a well.
> Except it would be real—a different sky.
> Then you could burrow down until you came
> To China! Oh, it's nothing like New Jersey.
> There's people, trees, and houses, and all that,
> But much, much different. Nothing looks the same."
>
> I went and got the trowel out of the shed.
> And sweated like a coolie all that morning,
> Digging a hole beside the lilac-bush,

Down on my hands and knees. It was a sort
Of praying, I suspect. I watched my hand
Dig deep and darker, and I tried and tried
To dream a place where nothing was the same.
The trowel never did break through to blue.

Before the dream could weary of itself
My eyes were tired of looking into darkness,
My sunbaked head of hanging down a hole.
I stood up in a place I had forgotten,
Blinking and staggering while the earth went round
And showed me silver barns, the fields dozing
In palls of brightness, patens growing and gone
In the tides of leaves, and the whole sky china blue.
Until I got my balance back again
All that I saw was China, China, China.

With Richard Wilbur and "Digging for China" we have
gone beyond mere mental images; we begin to enter the
realm of passive imagination, sparked by daydreams. Such
dreams take various forms: the hidden wish, the "what if,"
the escape from reality for a time. The passive imagination
lies between the reproductive and the creative. If carried
to the extreme, it is sometimes ridiculous, sometimes dangerous, because it leads to the world of hallucinations, a
world where one lives only in the imagination. But the
passive imagination can, if properly used, serve as a spring-
board to the true creative imagination where bits and pieces
of the past and of the present are utilized to create something
new and meaningful.

　　　　　—done with my schoolwork, I commence
　My real life: my arsenal, my workshop
　Opens, and in impotent omnipotence

I put on the helmet and the breastplate Pop
Cut out and soldered for me. Here is the shield
I sawed from beaver board and painted; here on top
The bow that only Odysseus can wield
And eleven vermilion-ringed, goose-feathered arrows.
(The twelfth was broken on the battlefield
When, searching among snap beans and potatoes,
I stepped on it.) Some dry weeds, a dead cane
Are my spears. The knife on the bureau's
My throwing-knife; the small unpainted biplane
Without wheels—that so often, helped by human hands,
Has taken off from, landed on, the counterpane—
Is my Spad.
    O dead list, that misunderstands
And laughs at and lies about the new live wild
Loves it lists! that sets upright, in the sands
Of age in which nothing grows, where all our friends are old,
A few dried leaves marked THIS IS THE GREENWOOD—
O arms that arm, for a child's wars, the child!

And yet they are good, if anything is good,
Against his enemies. . . .

It seems so patently simple, so obvious. Creative imagination can be restored through recognition that the "real
life" of the child must always come first and that it is only
after the schoolwork is done that this life begins. We will
never succeed until we separate what the child wisely knows
is learning—reading for meaning, language arts exercises,
rules of grammar, the whole gamut of skills and knowledge—from what is done for sheer pleasure: escape reading,
storytelling ballads, funny poems, writing that is truly creative and not some formula devised to teach language arts.

The child who writes "I wish I were in New York in a cow's head" or "I used to be a peanut but now I am a grape," writes to formula and prescription at best and lives forever in passive imagination at worst. His real workshop, along with Randall Jarrell's, opens only when he has sawed and painted with his own hands, found out how to match his goal, his Greenwood, with metaphor of his own choosing. He has needed help, of course. His father has had to cut out and solder the breastplate, that which is nearest to his heart, for him. But it is his choice that *dried* leaves mark the *Green*wood. Is this not a clue for us—teachers, parents, educators—that we may make the climate and provide the raw materials but that there is a point beyond which we can never trespass? And whenever we try to do so—to ask the child to fill in our blanks, to describe feelings, to rhyme with words we have chosen, to interpret as we would—we have cut off hope of really helping. The child has his arms to fight us, and fight us he will with *his* priorities for a "real life." And he learns it is not easy—as many would like to believe! But there is more.

Now as I was young and easy under the apple boughs
About the lilting house and happy as the grass was green,
    The night above the dingle starry,
        Time let me hail and climb
    Golden in the heydays of his eyes,
And honoured among wagons I was prince of the apple towns
And once below a time I lordly had the trees and leaves
        Trail with daisies and barley
    Down the rivers of the windfall light.

And as I was green and carefree, famous among the barns
About the happy yard and singing as the farm was home,

In the sun that is young once only,
    Time let me play and be
Golden in the mercy of his means. . . .

"Time let me play," says Dylan Thomas in "Fern Hill,"
much as William Blake and Lewis Carroll, fighting Dr. Isaac
Watts and the didactic moralists, said over and over again.
The sun is young once only; let there be dreams and food,
let there be play. It is the true nurse of *Songs of Innocence*
who allows the children to stay up beyond the usual hour;
the false nurse of *Songs of Experience* who tells them that

Your spring & your day are wasted in play.

If there is no free time, no dreams, and no play, there
can be no imagination; no one to dig to China, to arm
himself for battles in the Greenwood, to become prince
of the apple towns honored by wagons.

Mips and ma the mooly moo,
The likes of him is biting who,
A cow's a care and who's a coo?—
What footie does is final.

My dearest dear my fairest fair,
Your father tossed a cat in air,
Though neither you nor I was there,—
What footie does is final.

Theodore Roethke

Which one of us is willing to stand up for nonsense, for
apprehension at the expense of comprehension, for the
richness of words without a dictionary, for other sounds
that are never understood perhaps for a lifetime but whose
apprehension lives in the memory forever?

> The splendour falls on castle walls
>   And snowy summits old in story:
> The long light shakes across the lakes,
>   And the wild cataract leaps in glory.
> Blow, bugle, blow, set the wild echoes flying,
> Blow, bugle; answer, echoes, dying, dying, dying.

Alfred, Lord Tennyson

I believe that we can find a way once again to hear the wild echoes, to see a bear in a bush, to welcome Dinky and shut the door on Mr. Nobody, to spell out the names and habitats of the forms of things unknown. I believe that creative imagination can be restored by adventures that provide a glimpse of worlds beyond; by the sort of drama found only in good literature that portends the pleasure and the pain ahead; by hands that take up a vorpal sword, dig with a trowel, or saw a shield from beaver board. I believe that in the echoes and in the dried leaves there is music by which we can march against our enemies: humdrum existence and apathy; passive toys that give answers instead of questions; television that finds no room for private discovery and for passionate digression; mediocre books that masquerade as literature; audiovisual media that put a crimp in reading and verbal skills; ersatz creative writing that smacks of catalogs or encyclopedias or "spillage of raw emotion"; and classroom materials that make the *art of teaching* seem unnecessary and obsolete.

These enemies can be routed; creative imagination can return if we dig deeply, working with our hands and hearts to fashion the arms, the signs. There will be fatigue and hard work because, alas, there is no easy way—no magic pill—although there may be many false prophets always promising and offering it. For here are adventure, fantasies impossible in our mundane world, dreams to carry, and arms to bear against dull reason. And children know that when we try to mix our lessons and our reason with their real life, both suffer.

The present, Kornei Chukovsky writes, belongs to the sober, the cautious, and the routine-prone; but the future belongs to those who do not rein in their imaginations. And the use of imagination—creative imagination—enables children to become "fearless participants" in imaginary struggles for justice, goodness, and freedom, just as it enables us to answer to the struggles of reality. These we, too, have sensed since we were children; these we face now because of our deep commitment to the wonder and excitement of what is possible for them.

> Sometimes I envy those
> who spring like great black-
> and-gold butterflies
> before the crowded feet
> of summer—
>   brief, intense,
> like pieces of the sun,
> they are remembered and celebrated
> long after night has fallen.
>
> But I believe also in one
> who in the dead of winter
> tunnels through a damp,
> clinging darkness,
> nosing the soil of old gardens.

He lives unnoticed, but
deep within him there is a dream
of the surface one day
breaking and crumbling:

and a small, brown-furred
figure stands there,
blinking at the sky,
as the rising sun slowly dries
his strange, unruly wings.

John Haines

The Voice of the Poet

This was a Poet—
it is that
Distills amazing sense
From ordinary
Meanings,
And attars so immense

From the familiar species
That perished by the door,
We wonder it was not
Ourselves
Arrested it before.

Of pictures the discloser—
The Poet, it is he,
Entitles us by contrast
To ceaseless poverty.

Of portion so unconscious
The robbing could not harm.
Himself, to him, a fortune
Exterior to Time.

This poem by Emily Dickinson is one I have returned
to for many years in search of various clues, not least of

which is Dickinson's idea of the voice of poetry. It would seem to say that the poet finds and uses what to most people is commonplace, useless, and dead. This stuff of poetry, the sense and essence of life, is distilled and disclosed through a series of pictures, so vast that the poet gives them unconsciously and still retains more. These riches are so great, indeed, that they persist forever.

One clue to this belief lies in the first two lines:

> This *was* a poet—
> It *is* that

The change in tense indicates that although the poet *was*, his poetry still *is*, and the idea is carried forth to the last line, where we learn that his fortune is "exterior to Time." The striking words "arrest," "poverty," "robbing," and "fortune" suggest, furthermore, that the poet has the power to seize, to take into custody and catch hold of that which we cannot. We are poverty-stricken, and were we even to rob the poet, he would still have his fortune. Dickinson's view, therefore, leads us to regard ourselves as poor while the poet is rich. The poem gains in meaning if we think of a door as a symbol for access to something within. We would have to go through the door to commit our arrest or burglary, but the poet notices what lies dead *by* the door and takes what he needs without resorting to entrance. He is able to extract the attar, the essential oil from the "familiar species" that we left to perish.

The product of the poet's art is symbolism to which we may all respond in varying degree. The ghost of Hamlet's father is not easily erased from the mind or imagination. Those interested in visual art may well claim that the symbolism of Michelangelo or Warhol has an everlasting power. The novelist may assert that Tolstoy or Hemingway are supreme. The scientist may point to Einstein or Darwin, and the fantasy writer to Tolkien or Le Guin. Those drawn to music wage their own wars over Bach or Stravinsky. What we are all seeking in literature as well as in art and music are some answers to our human condition. "What matters," George Steiner wrote, "is truth and splendor of human experience in the light of conflict." That we are able to seek some measure of conciliation in our lives, some resolution to personal conflict, is one of the reasons for art itself.

We cannot, of course, hope to find this meaning in science. "Science," says I. A. Richards, "can tell us our place, but it cannot tell us what we are or what the world is about." For this knowledge we must turn to those arts that speak to our imaginations and emotions. They are all we have to keep us human. We cannot, on the other hand, ignore science. The twentieth century, like all eras, has its prophets of gloom and doom, and there is every chance we will be blown up along with our works of art. But it will *not* be because of what science has unleashed—it will be, in the end, because we have failed to respond with emotion and imagination and reason to things as they are, and reorder in new ways.

What we ask of art—any art—then, is that it appeal to our emotions, that we be allowed to use it to stretch our perceptions and adjust more fully to reality, that it in some way humanize us, and that, most important of all, it arrest us to such a degree that we emerge from our contact with it somewhat changed for the better, more aware of our possibilities and more fully able to resolve our conflicts.

We may be but temporarily arrested; indeed, it may only be illusion, but through this illusion we will see in a different light our own problems and triumph over our conflicts.

On the other hand, we may view the arts as some method for escape. We may wish to flee to the dream world of Walter de la Mare, to the primitive past devoid of contemporary evil of D. H. Lawrence, to a desert island with Defoe, to the never-never land of James Barrie or the bonneted and beribboned world of Kate Greenaway, to the tangled forests of Rackham. It does not really matter how we choose to view the arts and symbolism—as escape or as mind stretching. That they hold some solution to conflict is reason enough, and our individual choice of the specific art or genre within an art form bespeaks our own taste as individuals. Disney will do well for some; others demand sterner stuff.

We cannot, in other words, subsist by science alone, for what it tells us is *true* and verifiable, what it tells us is logical, and what it tells us is borne out through empiricism. But we are not wholly rational, logical entities; our ideas and emotions have a habit of being thoroughly mixed up. So whereas science makes, as we understand it, true assertions, art makes by its very nature quite a different sort of assertion. It invites us to lay aside pure fact, to dispense with that part of our lives guided by reason and enter temporarily a world where our emotions and imaginations may have free rein. There must, however, be enough of reality to make the symbols believable, enough consonant with our own experience that we can make a connection. Otherwise we are apt to dismiss the art as the ravings of a lunatic bound up only in personal symbolism and meanings to which we have no link.

What scientist, artist, and all of us must have, therefore, is some discernible order. Novelists may think of place, time, characters, and plot if they are to appeal to our imaginations and emotions. Writers of fantasy have high need of order for their imaginary worlds where all things within those worlds must function to some purpose. Artists must know how to arrange their lines and colors so that our eyes are drawn to what they wish us to see and do not spill off the canvas. Poets must arrange their words and images in some order we can follow. Not *all* orders appeal to all of us, but order is an essential of good art.

Poetic order has been expressed by various schools of poets in every century. Poetics in the traditional sense of the term is pitted quite vigorously today against the many new schools of poetry, which often find their expression in studied disorder. The chaos of present-day human experience is thought, by some, to be better expressed by open forms, with little attention to metrics, and certainly none to rhyme or established poetic devices, than in closed form, rhyme, and the classic symbolism of earlier poets.

The "academics" are clearly out of favor for many. Wordsworth's call for "natural language" and scenes close to nature has been taken up in native American ways, and the credit given to Pound, Williams, and Whitman. Eliot is out—subjectivity is in. Universal symbol is out—personal symbolism in. Metrics are out and "inspiration of the natural breath" is in. Objectivity is out—confession is in. The American vice, Horace Gregory wrote, is to "make all things new" without regard for the past. Some believe in imagination, some in the recalled unconscious, the fragmented psyche, while others keep their eye on object and still others on a faith in past civilizations or other less materialistic cultures, the domain of the "noble savage." Thus when we speak of poetry we are speaking of a variety of beliefs, truths, and styles, but inherent in all is that the order implied is based on a deeply felt view of the world that is intended to communicate a belief or a vision.

It is, of course, the same for the other arts. There are many schools of art, beliefs about the writing of fantasy, fiction, or realism. In each there is an order, and in each there is a statement made that is intended to answer questions science cannot, about "what we are and what the world is." Artists believe their statements to be true, although these statements cannot be proved empirically; these assertions, moreover, must be cast in an illusion consonant with the artists' emotions and imaginations—and ours. Call it a pseudostatement, call it a statement of illusion, call it a false statement; it is a statement and it must be dealt with.

To show this sort of statement in poetry, let us take Tennyson's "The Eagle."

> He clasps the crag with crooked hands;
> Close to the sun in lonely lands,
> Ringed with the azured world, he stands.
>
> The wrinkled sea beneath him crawls;
> He watches from his mountain walls,
> And like a thunderbolt he falls.

Certainly any logical, clear-thinking adult would have to doubt the veracity of the eagle as Tennyson shows him. An eagle does not have hands, nor can he get close to the sun. The sea is not wrinkled, nor does it crawl. Mountains do not have walls. Yet in Tennyson's view we see the eagle very clearly, and his false or pseudostatement would seem to be true. Tennyson has employed figurative language, personification, hyperbole, and a strict metrical iambic rhythm within the tercet form for his purpose and order. In a like manner this order and control is used by poets to direct the attention of their readers and listeners to what they wish to tell or show, as is seen in e. e. cummings's "hist whist."

Nowhere, it seems to me, is this order clearer and more discernible than in the poet who writes for children. For it is order directed to a special audience, intended to impart very clear beliefs about the *tabula rasa* of childhood and to make some very specific responses to "what we are and what the world is."

In English poetry there is only a small amount of verse directed to children before the end of the seventeenth century, due to the fact that children were considered nothing more than miniature adults who could partake of whatever literature was written. The few pieces that do exist, according to Iona and Peter Opie, "are always found to be attempts by the authors to ingratiate themselves with one or other of the parents, on the well-known principle that 'he who wipes the child's nose, kisseth the mother's cheek.'" The poetry, or verse, we do have is a catalog of admonitions to teach cleanliness, obedience, and various moral and religious values. Chaucer's "Controlling the Tongue" is of this ilk:

> My son, keep well thy tongue, and keep thy friend.
> A wicked tongue is worse than a fiend.
> My son, from a fiend men may them bless.
> My son, God of his endless goodness

> Walled a tongue with teeth and lips eke,
> For man should him avise what he speak . . .

Fifteenth-century verse exhorted children to courtesy, good manners, the avoidance of idleness and evil company, and in Robert Herrick's words to

> Honour thy parents; but good manners call
> Thee to adore thy God, the first of all.

But it was Dr. Isaac Watts, born in the seventeenth century, whose influence was to set in motion the rationale for children's verse. Ranting against "all the adventures of gods and heroes, all the dazzling images of false lustre that form and garnish a heathen song," he denounces the "licentious poems" that have waged open war with the pious design of church and state.

> The press has spread the poison far, and scattered wide the mortal infection: unthinking youth have enticed to sin beyond the vicious propensities of nature, plunged early into diseases and death, and sunk down to damnation in multitudes.

What Watts chose and wrote, instead, was

> dressing the scenes of religion in their proper figures of majesty, sweetness . . . creating power, of redeeming love, and renewing grace . . . an art, whose sweet insinuations might almost convey piety in reflecting nature, and melt the hardiest souls to the love of virtue.

These lessons, he wisely foresaw, would be best remembered if presented in rhyme so children could consign them to memory. And mighty lessons they were:

'Tis the voice of the sluggard, I heard him complain,
"You have wak'd me too soon, I must slumber again."
As the door on its hinges, so he on his bed,
Turns his sides and his shoulders and his heavy head.

"A little more sleep, and a little more slumber";
Thus he wastes half his days, and his hours without number,
And when he gets up he sits folding his hands,
Or walks about sauntering, or trifling he stands.

I pass'd by his garden, and saw the wild briar,
The thorn and the thistle grow broader and higher;
The clothes that hang on him are turning to rags;
And his money still wastes till he starves or he begs.

I made him a visit, still hoping to find
That he took better care for improving his mind:
He told me his dreams, talked of eating and drinking;
But he scarce reads his Bible, and never loves thinking.

Said I then to my heart, "Here's a lesson for me,"
This man's but a picture of what I might be;
But thanks to my friends for their care in my breeding,
Who taught me betimes to love working and reading.

And so the voice of the children's poet, consciously directed, began its own two main routes. On the one hand was the voice that valued the virtues of nature, of experience, of a pattern of life in accordance with reality, of proper behavior, and ultimately, attention to religious precepts. It was and is a highly moral view. On the other hand is the voice that took its roots in play, in imagination and dreams, in the innocent pleasures of life and even escape from the harsh realities of existence. This view is also moralistic, for it takes cognizance of the highly important role of play and imagination in life, of emotions and feelings that run counter to the established order of fact. At one end is Watts and his dutiful child, listening to the now-forgotten stanzas of his disciples, the Taylor sisters who urged children not to pull the cat's tail when all they listened to was "I love little pussy/Her coat is so warm." At the other is Lewis Carroll's Alice, reciting "Father William" all wrong, and the White Knight turning Wordsworth's "Resolution and Independence," with its deep philosophical speculations, into a mockery with

> I'll tell thee everything I can,
> There's *little* to relate.

There are, of course, many offshoots, where the emphasis shifts in favor of some aspect of the poet's beliefs. It is just this variation that lures readers to their favorite poets, their passions and prejudices. Those who consider Robert Louis Stevenson the first of the major children's poets do so, undoubtedly, because he understood the important nature of the "play-business" of children; their swings, their shadows, their lands of counterpanes. But there are those who balk (and justifiably so) at his xenophobia in "Foreign Children."

> Little Indian, Sioux or Crow,
> Little frosty Eskimo,
> Little Turk or Japanee,
> O! don't you wish that you were me?
>
> You have seen the scarlet trees
> And the lions over seas:
> You have eaten ostrich eggs,
> And turned the turtles off their legs.

Such a life is very fine,
But it's not so nice as mine:
You must often, as you trod,
Have wearied *not* to be abroad.

You have curious things to eat,
I am fed on proper meat;
You must dwell beyond the foam,
But I am safe and live at home.

Little Indian, Sioux or Crow,
Little frosty Eskimo,
Little Turk or Japanee,
O! don't you wish that you were me?

This chauvinism, however, is not unique to an Englishman of Stevenson's time. In a like manner Laura Richards in *Tirra-Lirra* pokes fun at the Chinese, the Russians, the French, and other foreigners. She renames Confucius, Confushy. She makes fun of American Indian names by inventing her own: Whopsy Whittlesey Whanko Whee, Wah-Wahbocky, Michiky Moo, and Squaw-Pan. This is not nonsense; it is not even humor; it is name-calling and an American form of xenophobia, just as distasteful. It goes beyond the respect for the changing of the guards at Buckingham Palace to be found in Milne; the patriotism displayed by the Benéts in *A Book of Americans*, Natalia Belting's interest in primitive beliefs; Arnold Adoff's adherence to the black and mixed family; the black experience as portrayed by June Jordan, Lucille Clifton, and Nikki Giovanni; and Eve Merriam's deep concern for transistors, neuter computers, TV commercials, and other imagination killers of our time. These are all voices of the moralist, directing children's attention to the dignity of all people, of famous persons, and to the deep values in which the poet believes.

The moralist view takes its turns and twists in many ways. Nature, as the model from which children should learn (as was stated so strongly in Rousseau's *Emile*), is in the voices of many contemporary poets: Aileen Fisher, Harry Behn, David McCord, and Lilian Moore, most notably. Nature as metaphor is pronounced in Valerie Worth. Science is emphasized in Lillian Morrison. Human nature and everyday experience are the realm of Karla Kuskin, Felice Holman, Kaye Starbird, and John Ciardi, to name but a few. Many children's poets encompass a wide range of models, leaving the dream world to William Allingham, Rose Fyleman, and Walter de la Mare. The emotional world of the child is explored by most children's poets, and there are still other byways. Whatever the emphasis, there is evidence of a highly moral view, but shorn of the didacticism that characterized eighteenth- and nineteenth-century children's verse.

Decrying the "fairy fictions of the last generation, which wandered over the region of shadows," Lucy Aikin wrote in 1831 of the rationale for her own anthology:

> By the aid of verse, a store of beautiful imagery and glowing sentiment may be gathered up as the amusement of childhood, which, in riper years, may soothe the heavy hours of languor, solitude and sorrow; may enforce sentiments of piety, humanity, and tenderness; may soothe the soul to calmness, rouse it to honourable exertion, or fire it with virtuous indignation.

Such didactic purposes have long been discarded except in the hands of the versifier. This is precisely where poets and the versifiers part company. Poets have respect for the child; the pseudostatements they use are geared to and show respect for the young. Versifiers talk down to the child. Their pseudostatements reside in cutesy metaphor that is both cloying and boring, and often they use no pseudostatement at all. Poets use meter and rhyme carefully, avoiding singsong rhythm and rhyme for its own sake. Poor versifiers do not even know the difference. Poets understand where the models lie to which children respond, and make use of them. Versifiers choose models they feel children should like because they are good for the children and—for fear they will overlook something, or because they cannot select and *order*—incorporate everything they know. Poets understand the difference between nonsense and light verse. Versifiers do not; they mix these up and offer their readers a convoluted package that is boring at best and destructive at worst.

One example of a versifier shows the difference between the versifier and the poet. The subject is friends or friendship.

> Our teacher says there is a rule
> We should remember while at school,
>
> At home, at play, what'er we do,
> And that's the rule of friendship true.
>
> If you would have friends, you must do
> To them the kindly things that you
>
> Would like to have them do, and say
> To you while at your work or play.
>
> And that's the rule of friendship true;
> It works in all we say and do.

It pays to be a friend polite
For friendship's rule is always right.

There is no pseudostatement here, no metaphor, nothing but a sanctimonious message in metrically perfect iambic tetrameter with no model but the teacher. At least Dr. Watts gave us a bee!

If there are lessons to be learned, they are—in the hands of good poets—bereft of the "thou shalt" and "thou shalt not." As stylists, the best poets find other ways, and if they feel an irresistible urge to hammer a message home, the poets will share in the burden of proof. Eve Merriam is a past master at this technique. A cliché, she explains, is

> what we all say
> when we're too lazy
> to find another way.

She avoids pointing an accusing finger by playing a dual role both as poet and reader. Writing of "it" and "they," she comments that

> THEY just make it all up,
> and "we" go along.

By becoming a part of the "we," the child is never censured. Wordplay is used by a number of poets as a foil for didacticism, and meter and rhyme are called in to help by most. In that, Dr. Watts has triumphed.

Wordplay is the stock in trade of a handful of poets who write for children, but wordplay and wit are seen most frequently in those poets who choose to stress the play aspects of children. Wit is predominant in Hilaire Belloc, whose spoofs on the *Struwwelpeter* cautionary rhyme have been loved for years. Richard Wilbur uses wit in *Opposites*. N. M. Bodecker and X. J. Kennedy are masters of wit. It appears in McCord, Ciardi, and Merriam to a lesser degree.

To understand this second major voice used by children's poets, that of play, imagination, dreams, and escape, it is important to make a distinction between what is humor and light verse and witty, and what is pure nonsense. For although they use the same tools—wordplay, wit, impossible human aberrations, personification, inversions, neologisms, strange juxtapositions, language distortion, hyperbole, and alliteration—there are striking dissimilarities and differences.

Nonsense is lawless; it is a realm where the physical laws of nature are broken. Its very purpose is to rebel against reason; indeed, it is a defiance of reason. It uses the stuff of reality but it transfers it through very careful and logical order to an impossible world, a world that poses no threats because it does not take into consideration our real emotions and feelings. We are able to enter the world of nonsense and enjoy it, in other words, because it poses no threat to our normal feelings. It does not mirror those feelings and emotions as a work of fantasy does (where good must win over evil) because in the nonsense writer's world there is no evil or good. In nonsense, then, we can make a real escape, without fear that we will become emotionally involved. For this reason, nonsense is not easily written.

We do not care, for example, if Edward Lear's limerick characters have noses ten feet long or a lady's chin is so sharp she can use it to play on her harp. We laugh! In the world of reality such a nose or chin is an impossibility; such aberrations defy nature. Were we to know someone, however, who had an unsightly nose or a very sharp chin, we would be apt to feel sorry for that person. If we are lacking in sensibility, we might make fun of these unfortunate features and write a piece of light verse about them, but it would *not* be nonsense because it would involve our true feelings. It takes an unusually high degree of order and an ultimate craftsmanship to write true nonsense.

Now this is precisely the difficulty. For there are two things happening in the voice of children's poets today—although it would be better to call them versifiers (and not poets)—that would seem to me to break the long tradition of morality in writing for children, a morality that has pervaded this field for many centuries.

The first occurs in taking established nonsense and embellishing it with purpose. To do so is to destroy its value. Such an act negates the very belief in the need for imagination and play and dream of the child and takes us right back to Watts. Watts's archbigotry is not to be forgiven, but he did not, in all fairness, have the advantage of knowing what psychology has taught us about the healthful aspects of play and imagination. Those who write today *should* know better! One does not admire Disney for turning Pinocchio's talking cricket into a song-and-dance man and thus negating the symbolism of conscience. Nor does one admire those who water down fairy tales, again destroying the symbolism of universal values that have long helped humanity to resolve conflicts. It is impossible, therefore, for me to ignore those who tamper with the pseudostatement of poetry to the degree that they disturb morality itself and divest children of their need for nonsense. For in this view, in the name of a religious morality, the greater morality is destroyed. Three blind mice become three "church mice," the ten little Indians become ten little "missionaries," the three men in a tub are transformed to three little boys "scrubbing and rubbing/To please their mommy, you see." The pussy cat does not go to London to see the Queen and frighten a little mouse, but meets the Queen of Sheba and wise King Solomon. The muffin man sells manna bread. Old King Cole calls "for the Lord/to save his soul" while the fiddlers three have a "fine fiddle ministry" of "song and prayers." One no longer asks "How many miles to Babylon?" but "How many miles to Bethlehem?" Old Mother Hubbard need never go searching for bones because God has put plenty in a sack for her dog. Pat-a-cakes are marked with *G* for God. Tom takes back the pig because God tells him to. Tweedledum and Tweedledee say "I'm sorry" instead of quarreling, and Jesus brings back Little Bo-Peep's lost sheep. But most immoral of all—those that give the child no guidelines, no symbols, no handles with which to come to grips with the world as it is, and destroy not only nonsense but reality itself—are such purported "spiritual" offerings as:

> There was a crooked man
> 　Who walked a crooked mile.
> He never could straighten up,
> 　So never did smile.
> He found a little book
> 　That said "God makes
> The crooked straight!"
> 　He believed
> And straightened up with smiles
> 　And jumped the golden gate!

As a contrast to this sort of immorality, consider Shel Silverstein, who is very much in tune with children and with what Rousseau called children's innate goodness. His verse is highly moral in every respect. He understands the catalog of human foibles to which children respond and of which they are aware, from being afraid of the dark to nagging to impoliteness to laziness. He is all for imagination; he believes in putting

> something silly in the world
> That ain't been there before.

He abhors war and the imagination killers of our age, and invents justifiable ends for those prone to evil. He believes that no matter what color our faces are by day "we are all the same when we turn off the light"; that we need to polish stars and, indeed, that children alone know where the sidewalk ends. His morality is expressed in a myriad of ways; if he errs in being a bit didactic at times, his humor saves him from being a disciple of Watts.

> If we meet and I say, "Hi,"
> That's a salutation.
> If you ask me how I feel,
> That's consideration.
> If we stop and talk awhile,
> That's a conversation.
> If we understand each other,
> That's communication.
> If we argue, scream and fight,
> That's an altercation.
> If later we apologize,
> That's reconciliation.
> If we help each other home,
> That's cooperation.

And all these ations added up
Make civilization.

(And if I say this is a wonderful poem,
Is that exaggeration?)

To be frank, it is exaggeration, because Silverstein is not
really a poet, but a light versifier. He uses none of the
refinements of figurative language, and his metrical structure
is often shoddy. But his morality shines, and in that he
carries out a long and respected tradition.

The second immorality that is insidiously creeping into
children's verse is far removed from the sanction of religion,
and is probably less noticed because it pretends to treasure
play and imagination, but in actuality distorts it and negates
its positive value. It is deceptive in appearance because it
employs all the skilled craft of the poet, the figurative language, the wordplay, and it is filled with pseudostatement.
It pays attention to the same foibles of human nature that
Silverstein employs, but its tone is quite the opposite. It
delights in aberrations, both of human physiology and behavior. It takes pleasure in the gross and baser side of
human nature and invests it with a morality of its own. It
has an obsessive concern with gluttony, obesity, sadism,
nastiness, selfishness. Its heroes, with ostensibly foolish and
nonsensical names, destroy each other by sheer overweight
or by eating each other. Its rollicking rhythms mask the
fact that there is never any comeuppance for those who
are sadistic and mean. It pokes fun at those with physical
deformities, at those who wish to study or fit into the establishment, and it portrays women as dumb, foolish, addled,
and good for only one thing: to cook in the kitchen. In
addition, it conjures up a host of monsters, giants, trolls,

vampires, wizards, and other nonworldly specters who glory in death and fear. While this all stems from the idea that children enjoy imaginary creatures and enjoy being frightened, it presents the creatures as so all-powerful that the child is left with no means to attack or fight them. They are not models in nature, in human nature, but in nightmare. They present conflict with no solution.

To understand this lack of morality is to recall a long tradition of poets who use pseudostatement as a means of entering the emotions and feelings of reader and listener. If we believe that what matters for children, as for ourselves, is the truth and splendor of human experience in the light of conflict, and that in literature we will find out what we are and what the world is about, we must similarly believe that to destroy the pseudostatement of poetry (or any art), the illusion and joy of Mother Goose's nonsense, by interjecting a religious motif that makes all things good and right, negates not only the conflict but also the very nature of our need for nonsense.

> A man in the wilderness asked me
> How many strawberries grow in the sea.
> I answered him as I thought good
> As many red herrings as grow in the wood.

Children hearing this will think to themselves—How foolish! We know better than that. Strawberries cannot grow in the sea, nor fishes in the wood. How smart we are to know this!

But what of the children who read or hear Marjorie Decker's version:

> The man in the wilderness
>   Said to me,

"How many children
   Walked through the Red Sea?"
I answered him
   As I thought I should
"As many as God said there would."

These children are asked a question that is not only inappropriate for their age but unanswerable by the most scholarly theologian. Worse than that, it destroys the very nature of the value of nonsense, by allowing no room for imagination and by making them feel stupid. By removing the nonsense, children's growth of consciousness is completely altered; they are asked to deal with both a reality that is false because there is no answer and a logic for which no one is prepared, least of all children. They cannot, in short, triumph over conflict because the conflict itself is false.

Similarly, to lock children into a world where they see nothing but aberrations is to deny them the tools to solve that conflict, to deny them the right to hope and to find those tools, whether within themselves or in models of nature or with the help of a trusted adult.

> The thing about a shark is—teeth,
> One row above, one row beneath.
>
> Now take a close look. Do you find
> It has another row behind?
>
> Still closer—here, I'll hold your hat:
> Has it a third row behind that?
>
> Now look in and . . . Look out! Oh my,
> I'll *never* know now! Well, goodbye.
>
>   John Ciardi

It is obvious that the tone of this poem is a playful one; the narrator, in asking questions by degrees, prepares the reader for what is obviously a foolish occupation: to count— if one could get close enough to do so—the teeth of sharks. But children know the thing is impossible, and even if it were not, there is the company of someone else at hand.

> I have a purple dragon
> With a long brass tail that clangs,
> And anyone not nice to me
> Soon feels his fiery fangs,
>
> So if you tell me I'm a dope
> Or call my muscles jelly,
> You might just dwell a billion years
> Inside his boiling belly.
>
>   X. J. Kennedy

Again, the tone is playful; the idea of a purple dragon with a bell on the end of his tail is nonsense. Yet even if children do not recognize it as such, they know that by being kind to the narrator they can avoid being eaten by the dragon.

> Elevator operator
> P. Cornelius Alligator,
> when his passengers
> were many,
> never
> ever
> passed up
> any:
> when his passengers
> were few,
> always managed

to make do.
When they told him:
"Mister 'Gator!
quickly
in your elevator
take us
to the nineteenth floor!"
they were never
seen no more.

N. M. Bodecker

Here again, the concept of an alligator as an elevator operator falls into the category of nonsense, and the light tone of the narrator removes the verse from any immediate threat to the reader. But even should children, in some unforeseen way, decide that an elevator operator was indeed an alligator, they would still have the choice of riding either with trusted adults or not getting into the elevator at all.

The gruesome ghoul, the grisly ghoul,
without the slightest noise
waits patiently beside the school
to feast on girls and boys.

He lunges fiercely through the air
as they come out to play,
then grabs a couple by the hair
and drags them far away.

He cracks their bones and snaps their backs
and squeezes out their lungs,
he chews their thumbs like candy snacks
and pulls apart their tongues.

He slices their stomachs and bites their hearts
and tears their flesh to shreds,
he swallows their toes like toasted tarts
and gobbles down their heads.

Fingers, elbows, hands and knees
and arms and legs and feet—
he eats them with delight and ease,
for every part's a treat.

And when the gruesome, grisly ghoul
has nothing left to chew,
he hurries to another school
and waits . . . perhaps for you.

                                   Jack Prelutsky

This poem, however, presents a different view, for its narrator offers no hope, or means of fighting or outwitting an otherworldly creature, short of staying home from school. To be perfectly fair, its genre suggests that giants, mummies, krakens, elves and will-o'-the-wisps, dragons, ogres, skeletons, and specters can be avoided if children do not go near dark caverns, deserts, oceans, forests, woods, graveyards, or moors. But an open window in a home invites the vampire, a "pleasant stroll" makes children prey to a meal for a troll, werewolves roam the streets, invisible beasts stalk the parks, witches and headless horsemen roam the skies, and zombies, banshees, and poltergeists inhabit the houses and bedrooms:

And you shiver and you scream
for you know it's not a dream
as the zombie nears your bed.

To listen to those adults who say that children know this is all in fun may be prudent. But the experience of dealing with children over many years, weathering out the initial reaction to *Where the Wild Things Are*, a book that gave the children a vent to their imaginations but also offered them a "magic trick of staring into all their yellow eyes without blinking once," knowing that children go through stages when they do not want to go up dark stairs or go out on Halloween without trusted adults, convinces me that this voice in poetry is an immoral voice because, rather than allaying conflicts and fears, it fosters them. Children need the "magic tricks," and to withhold them is an immorality.

The voice of the poet, the children's poet, is a powerful voice. It can help the young to know something of the "truth and splendor in the light of conflict" and it has, traditionally, chosen two paths, both equally important: that of realism and that of imagination. It has stretched perceptions, made children aware of possibilities, and fostered a spirit of trust. Through nature and reality, it has encouraged growth of consciousness; through imagination and nonsense it has given children a measure of their own worth. To destroy that important need for nonsense and dream is immoral. To offer the child no guide to help him through the conflict and to state the conflict in terms of fear, to destroy order, is also immoral.

The voice of the poet is also a conscious voice. It cannot take refuge in the chaos of the unconscious, for if it does children will have no chance to know what they are or what the world is. Children must have the opportunity to "distill sense from ordinary meaning," to make their own pictures. They must not be left in "ceaseless poverty," but given their full portion of the "familiar species." With rare exception, the voice of the poet has given them this chance.

ON LITERATURE

Literature, Creativity, and Imagination

Of all the inventions dreamed up by man, none seems more pertinent to the topic of "Literature, Creativity, and Imagination" than those remarkable devices fashioned by the White Knight in *Through the Looking Glass, and What Alice Found There.*

You may remember them—a queer-shaped little deal box, in which to keep clothes and sandwiches, hung by a harness across the shoulders, and carried upside down so that the rain should not get in, discovered by Alice, curiously enough, with the lid wide open and the contents lost; another box, a mousetrap, fastened to the horse's saddle, in the event that any mice should happen to scamper up onto the horse; and anklets for the horse's feet "to guard against the bite of sharks." The list goes on—but the point, it seems to me, is quite evident. It is easy to laugh at the bungling White Knight, always tumbling off his horse "first on one side and then on the other"; but should we, on reading or remembering, label his inventions as sheer nonsense?

Lewis Carroll was a man who used nonsense as a very

special tool; his humor essentially turned logic upside down much as the White Knight, himself, thought better when falling, head downward, from his horse. "Nonsense," writes Phyllis Greenacre, one of Carroll's biographers, "is not only the lack of reason or expected order, but it is the defiance of reason which men value most, and it is achieved by apparent isolation, inconsequence, and generally heedless disconnection. There is a quality of (generally quiet) explosive destructiveness about sheer nonsense—an unannounced nihilism—which is never absolutely achieved to be sure, but is felt in its subtle implications."

Would it be rash to suggest, in speaking of creativity and imagination through literature, that these inventions, on closer examination, are not so nonsensical as first they seem? "To be funny," George Orwell wrote, "you have to be serious." And Lewis Carroll, the Reverend Charles Lutwidge Dodgson, was intensely serious about matters of the imagination, including the White Knight and his unusual inventions. It is to be wondered, rather, if we, living in an environment that pays lip service to the importance of imagination and creativity, are not the ones who may well seem nonsensical.

Let us start with the box the White Knight kept harnessed around his shoulders, close to the face and hands so that food and clothing were easily available. Symbolic, certainly, of the physical needs by which the human body is sustained, protected by being carried upside down so that the elements do not spoil these essentials for very life. Perhaps you will remember the Knight's reaction when Alice discovers the lid is unhinged and the contents scattered; immediately he hangs the empty box upon the branch of a tree, "in hopes some bees may make a nest in it—then I should get the honey."

Should you be able to accept my own thesis, that what Lewis Carroll did throughout his Alice books was to substitute, time and again, actual food for the body and the stomach for what we call "food for thought" or "food for the mind" (much as Maurice Sendak has, in a sense, more recently done), you will be able to envision that within this box of "food for thought" is that which we call literature, those words and ideas of permanent and universal interest that sustain the mind and emotion of both adult and child. Do we not keep this literature close to our heads, our eyes, and our hands, that we may easily pick up the books that enclose the words?

We know that in this literature is the power to stimulate, to strengthen the imaginations of our young people, to arouse curiosity, to develop creativity; and yet do we offer it, *really* offer it, at all? Indeed we categorize it, label it, make lists of it; our minds have logically arranged all this, and we have even built larger boxes called libraries. But what we have often failed to do is to recognize that the mind and logic do not, in themselves, assure successful use of the books, the words. "The mind alone cannot make sense of images," Archibald MacLeish tells us of poetry, "but emotions can—feelings can."

I am suggesting that we have become so consumed with the technicalities of the literature we offer that we often fail to read, really read, the text to understand with our hearts what it is saying. We have obliterated entire areas of exploration and substituted, when we speak of originality and creativity, mass-produced feelings and responses. Worse still, we have mistaken the tools and techniques, the forms, those things that should serve as the utensils and dishes for serving the food, the books, for the food itself. We have shied away from developing original thought and stretching the imagination; we have been fearful of emotions, of feelings; and the result is masses of so-called creative writing done by our children without the slightest glimmer of real creation.

In Randall Jarrell's *The Bat-Poet*, you will remember that the bat admires the songs of the mockingbird. The mockingbird has consented to listen to a poem that the bat has written about an owl who almost killed him. The bat eagerly awaits the mockingbird's response to the poem.

> "Why, I like it," said the mockingbird. "Technically, it's quite accomplished. The way you change the rhyme-scheme's particularly effective."
>
> The bat said, "It is?"
>
> "Oh yes," said the mockingbird. "And it was clever of you to have that last line two feet short."
>
> The bat said blankly: "Two feet short?"
>
> "It's two feet short," said the mockingbird a little impatiently. "The next-to-last-line's iambic pentameter, and the last line's iambic trimeter."
>
> The bat looked so bewildered that the mockingbird said in a kind voice: "An iambic foot has one weak syllable and one strong syllable; the weak one comes first. That last line of yours has six syllables and the one before it has ten: when you shorten the last line like that it gets the effect of the night holding its breath."
>
> "I didn't know that," the bat said. "I just made it like holding your breath."

"To be sure, to be sure!" said the mockingbird. "I enjoyed your poem very much. When you've made up some more do come round and say me another."

The bat said that he would, and fluttered home to his rafter. Partly he felt very good—the mockingbird had liked his poem—and partly he felt just terrible. He thought: "Why, I might as well have said it to the bats. What do I care about how many feet it has? The owl nearly kills me, and he says he likes the rhyme-scheme!"

Later, the bat has occasion to say the poem to a chipmunk, hoping to interest him in his own portrait in verse "for only six crickets."

> A shadow is floating through the moonlight.
> Its wings don't make a sound.
> Its claws are long, its beak is bright.
> Its eyes try all the corners of the night.
>
> It calls and calls: all the air swells and heaves
> And washes up and down like water.
> The ear that listens to the owl believes
> In death. The bat beneath the eaves,
>
> The mouse beside the stone are still as death—
> The owl's air washes them like water.
> The owl goes back and forth inside the night,
> And the night holds its breath.

He said his poem and the chipmunk listened attentively; when the poem was over the chipmunk gave a big shiver and said, "It's terrible, just terrible! Is there really something like that at night?"

Later the bat starts on his portrait in verse about the chipmunk.

But somehow he kept coming back to the poem about the owl, and what the chipmunk had said, and how he'd looked. "*He* didn't say any of that two-feet short stuff," the bat thought triumphantly; "*he* was scared."

How many mockingbirds fail to be scared—to sense the force that elicits emotion and imagination? How many teachers, so concerned with the rhyme scheme, the rhythm, accept these tools as substitutes for the meaning? How many little bats, how many children, must keep their poems and flights of imagination to themselves because there is a mockingbird so puffed up with his own song, his own dictates, that the real stuff of creation never gets through? I am reminded of any number of articles written by well-meaning teachers who pay lip service to the idea that poetry is made up of all the elements of life, yet who painstakingly elaborate on "themes" (nature, picnics, pets, holidays) they feel "suitable" for poetry. Heaven forbid that their students should venture off into realms that depart from the teacher's prescribed ideas of "Beauty" and "Truth"!

How many teachers have taken to their hearts a volume of children's poems called *Miracles*? It is very pleasant to read, for the beauties of nature are extolled on every page; it is what adults want to hear. But in how many other children do there burn more important, urgent things to feel and say? How many have seized upon the haiku, with its apt nature symbols, as a sop for counting out seventeen syllables (which is only a little better than an exercise in mathematics), never concerned with the meaning of the word "hokku," or "beginning phrase," which is the essence of the poem? How many more have recently set the children to busily turning out cinquains, another syllable-counting exercise?

How many have overworked Mary O'Neill's *Hailstones and Halibut Bones* as an exercise in having children write out red is a fire engine, blue is the ocean, green is the tree, ad infinitum? How many have spent endless hours praising such drivel as "The cat ate the fat bat and slept in a hat and that was that"?

None of this is creativity and imagination. It is but a mass-produced easy way out; and it concentrates on the form, the techniques, rather than on the force that burns in the child's mind and imagination and will never, at this rate, find a way to express itself.

Creativity and imagination are not built and fostered by these gimmicks. It is emotion and feeling that release creativity. To encourage in our children these qualities requires the sort of commitment made by an individual teacher who is willing to dip into the box and ferret out that which may be meaningful to each individual child. Such a commitment is made by encouraging different varieties of expression, by the recognition that each child will approach that which is read differently; it is built by the trust between child and teacher that nothing is alien to the emotions and imagination and that children will not be turned away because they have written something "unsuitable" in the teacher's judgment.

For some children, who, like the little bat, are born with the acute sensitivity that separates them from their peers, the release may be Randall Jarrell's *The Bat-Poet*; for this book will say to them that they are different, that such sensitivities do often alienate one in the beginning and such a person is inclined to be dubious and doubtful about the technicalities.

For another it may be such a book as Maurice Sendak's

Higgledy Piggledy Pop!, for children may well put themselves into the role of the dog, Jennie, bored by material
comforts, alienated by immaturity and lack of experience,
yearning to become a Leading Lady, and plunging, therefore,
into the perils of the world and Castle Yonder. Yet for
another it may be the very real story of Micucu, in Elizabeth
Bishop's *Ballad of the Burglar of Babylon*, running from
the police, a man alienated because he has flouted the
rules of society.

Without dwelling on the various aspects of personal and
social awareness within these books, I would only point
out that there is, in all three, the potential for identification.
The bat, the dog, the man all wish to be part of their world;
yet each is alienated, each faces the fears of his society—a
bat-eating owl, a lion, and a gun. Is it the mind alone—
reason, logic—or is it creativity and imagination that make
the bat turn his fear of death into a poem, that inspire the
words that Jennie uses to save Baby from the lion, and
that cause Micucu to settle for ninety hours on the hills of
Babylon although his death is certain? For each the experience is different.

I should like to interject here that lack of experience,
which we presume to be common to all children, just starting
in life, is one of the most germinal factors one can think
of for creativity and imagination. A young mind, unhampered
by clichés, by staid and oftentimes outmoded rules, can
put into new relationships the stuff of the world
he sees. Yet how often is this fresh approach squelched;
how often is the child's imagination made subservient to
techniques, forms?

Let me add quickly that I am far from opposed to forms,

to the proper training and use of the tools of the craft, but I feel they come second to the content, the meaning, the force. At the risk of repeating myself for the thousandth time, I should like to offer that one does not teach a child imagination or originality or how to write creatively. One only establishes the climate, the relationship with the world through literature, that helps children develop their sensitivities and introduces them gradually to the forms and craft in which imagination will find expression. The trouble is, as I see it today, that too many teachers are willing to accept the tools and techniques of creative writing for the real thing. They will dig no deeper than insisting a haiku have seventeen syllables—not fifteen, not nineteen—and making certain that "cat" rhymes with "hat," and that whatever thoughts or words come in between be correctly spelled and legibly written on neatly lined paper.

What, then, if we discard the gimmicks and turn back to the box of literature? What, then, if we commit ourselves to the imagination of each individual child who enters our classroom or library? "It is," says George Steiner, "a matter of seriousness and emotional risk, a recognition that the teaching of literature, if it can be done at all, is an extraordinarily complex and dangerous business, of knowing that one takes in hand the quick of another human being."

We must find new ways, new methods by which we may bring literature to our young people. For me poetry, as the literature of heightened consciousness, is one way of touching the individual child, finding the poem that sings in the child's own rhythm, offering in Stephen Spender's words "an event individually experienced" but with the knowledge that "this uniqueness is the universal mode of experiencing all events. Poetry makes one realize that one is alone, and complex; and that to be alone is universal."

For you, there will be hundreds of ways, based on your own feelings as to what a piece of literature strikes in you, as an individual, and therefore, one hopes, in the individual child. With this approach there can be no room for gimmickry and gimcracks, no mass-produced exercises in creative futility.

The White Knight, you see, had his own way. He turned the box upside down and left the lid open. What spilled along the way could be picked up by a passerby, and he could then hang the empty box on a tree so that it would be replenished by the bees with more "honey." Remember, too, the mousetrap box, perched upon the horse's saddle. It is, perhaps, unlikely that many mice will climb up a horse's leg; but on the off chance that it might happen, there is always the cheese.

As for the anklets around the horse's feet, to ward off any sharks, perhaps we ought to claim them and wind them around our own ankles. It is not nonsensical to envision that we may have great need of them, for when we step into new waters we are likely to upset many a heretofore cherished notion about literature and creativity and imagination. This I can promise you.

> Whenever the [Knight's] horse stopped (which it did often) he fell off in front; and, whenever it went on again (which it generally did rather suddenly), he fell off behind. Otherwise, he kept on pretty well, except that he had a habit of now and then falling off sideways; and, as he generally did this on the side on which Alice was walking, she soon found that it was the best plan not to walk *quite* close to the horse.

"I'm afraid you've not had much practice in riding," she ventured to say, as she was helping him up from his fifth tumble.

The Knight looked very much surprised, and a little offended at the remark. "What makes you say that?" he asked, as he scrambled back into the saddle, keeping hold of Alice's hair with one hand, to save himself from falling over on the other side.

"Because people don't fall off quite so often, when they've had much practice."

"I've had plenty of practice," the Knight said very gravely; "plenty of practice!"

Children's Literature— A Creative Weapon

It was particularly interesting for me recently to come across, in a book of excerpts from the notebooks of the American poet Theodore Roethke, an observation I should like to share with you. "It is wise," he wrote, "to keep in touch with chaos." I doubt that any of us, at times, are not visited by what the dictionary calls "a state of utter confusion or disorder," and we should not be surprised if historians one day characterize this particular time in history as one of chaos.

We know that when this chaos occurs, however, it does not do so in a vacuum; it is not just a matter of war or politics or religious upheaval, moral or ethical changes; the confusion seems to spill into all areas, and indeed into the sanctum sanctorum of children's literature. One has only to be aware of the past twenty years of this body of literature to realize that people concerned with children's reading and their books, united prior to that time for the most part as to standards for the books, are now caught up in polemics that rival any political platform.

What needs emphasis in Roethke's observation is that

we pay strict attention to the verbal phrase he has chosen: "keep in touch with."

This presupposes, of course, that disorder and confusion exist. There are, alas, many people living today (although sometimes I wonder if they are merely existing) who refuse to recognize chaos; who would have the world just as it was, in some permanent state of seeming perfection, who will always long for the good old days when everything sat prim and proper in its little niche. I am not sure what kind of Utopia this was, but I can imagine it was sometime around my own childhood. There were Hans Christian Andersen, Cinderella, Aesop, the Brothers Grimm, and although there were children like Tom and Huck, who were naughty, and Toad, who was irascible, and Alice, who was inclined to argue, and stepsisters who were self-centered and jealous, still and all their sins were not too wicked. They were, after all, merely human, or humanized, and to be forgiven.

Children respected their parents, strove for good grades, were taught right from wrong, enjoyed the saintliness of Shirley Temple, gobbled their Wheaties like Jack Armstrong, and ate their spinach like Popeye. Everybody, in fact, had the chance to go west and find Daddy Warbucks.

So it was probably some sort of idyllic world, apart from the crisis of the American economy. The worst that could happen to a child was a few nights of nightmares over the Lindbergh kidnapping or the sight of Disney's wicked stepmother in *Snow White and the Seven Dwarfs*. But Hauptmann and stepmother got their comeuppance, and we went on running through the hose in the summer and sledding in the winter, and our parents survived the

Depression, as somehow we will survive inflation today.

Would we, I must ask, want to go back? To re-create that bit of nostalgia that one can see very concisely today at Disneyland? To ride the two-decker bus, the horse and buggy, the trolley? To live in small communities, apart from the world at large, and cherish our provincialism?

Shall we turn back time, avoiding all that has happened to broaden the world, to dignify all men, to raise us up as more enlightened humans? True, this education has given rise to much disorder, much confusion, but would any of us, given the choice, write the words "It is wise to *avoid* chaos"?

Could any of us who work with children, who live in this world today, honestly wish to turn our backs on the necessity for questions, for arguments through which we have to struggle to go yet another step forward?

We can, of course, do just that. There is such a vast body of literature available to us that we are perfectly free to cull out what we don't like. We can find plenty of books in which Mother Goose has been altered to suit the didacticism and principles of health faddists, religious fanatics, and their ilk.

We can help out poor Miss Muffet by changing the spider into something more palatable for the young, such as a sweet little pussy cat. We can eliminate frightening Bible stories from the Sunday-school curriculum—Daniel in the Lion's Den and Jonah in the Whale. We can find any number of versions of Little Red Riding Hood where the wolf regurgitates Grandmother, thus sparing the child any fears.

No, Virginia, the Big Bad Wolf didn't eat up the two lazy pigs. He was only just pretending. It's all right to play and dance and sing all day and build flimsy houses and leave all the work to your brother. Nothing bad will ever happen to you; there will always be others around to use their wits and help you out. Life can be very simple, and anyone who tells you that another Hitler can rise up, or that a bomb can destroy you, is just making it up.

To choose this sort of watered-down diet of books, instead of the real literature, is perhaps to avoid chaos, for the moment. But whom do we cheat but the child, and indeed, eventually, ourselves? For many centuries we have had, close at hand, a body of literature that deals in the symbolisms of good and evil, a depersonalization of experience that has helped men of all ages better to understand and meet the hordes of problems that may affect their lives. Far more, it has given them optimism and hope that heroes slay ogres and princesses need not languish in towers forever.

When we bring into our schools and libraries ersatz monsters who cringe with fear at the sight of a five-year-old, we are pretending that chaos and disorder are really subjects for humor; monsters, in whatever guise, are not important and don't matter. It is, of course, commendable to face our problems with a sense of self-humor, but is it not humor misplaced when the evils themselves become objects for scorn? Chaos is not really a matter for derision.

Avoiding the idea that disorder exists in the world of children's books is quite harmful. In its most primary form it puts into motion the process of watering down the folk and fairy tale, removing the necessary symbolism, and thereby cheating our children of the right to know that there are matters of courage, of fortitude, of wit available to them to fight the evils that exist, sometimes with help from others and sometimes alone, or the evils that may come to pass.

Speaking of the Here-and-Now School of the 1920s in this country, which held that fantasy and folktale should be abolished, Lewis Mumford tells us, "We did not get rid of the dragon; we only banished St. George." In its other aspects it goes so far as to censor the right of the author or artist; it pretends that things remain at status quo.

In between the two extremes lie the safe books. They take many forms, but one of their chief appeals is the sort of sentimental approach to the past; their text is one of aphorisms and their illustrations depict children in bland pastels, quaintly dressed, children who are models of all virtues. There is nothing to criticize in these books except that they ignore the fact that anything current or new is going on; an occasional reviewer will attack them, crying for some identification with the city (usually New York), or objecting to the fact that in their niceties they ignore the real problems of life.

The other range of books is a raft of slim volumes of poetry—or verse. They extol the virtues of nature for the most part, of pleasant pastoral moments, and oftentimes range worldwide for the back-to-the-simple-life sort of approach. They are always lavishly illustrated, making up for what they lack in content and careful, thoughtful editing. Again there is nothing wrong with them except that they do not give a broad picture of the world as it is today.

But neither do I feel, as some do, that we should rewrite the observation to read, "It is wise to embrace chaos." It seems to me that lately many writers and publishers have jumped on a wagon that is headed for a fiery hell of "anything goes." Books written and published under this aegis take a special delight in picturing the shabbiest, most down-trodden, antimoral and antiethical looks at our society possible. It is as though all values of the past have been thrown overboard; nothing seems worth saving. Any sort of language, and/or diction, is permissible—any sort of mor-bid situation or scene to elicit the great shock value is emphasized.

More frightening than anything is the tendency of the writer to get his licks in at the establishment, to try to prove that all adults and their values are worthless. They side with the few members of the young in our society who feel that nothing is valid and least of all anything ex-pounded by anyone over the age of twenty. This is not actually said in so many words but it is felt, not alone in the conversations of the young (which may be accurate journalism) but more seriously intoned by the writer, who seems unable to find any redeeming feature in any adult. The same sort of thing is also happening in some of the writing by children that publishers push at us in glee; the city is terrible, people are awful, there is nothing to redeem the world.

Somewhere in between these two positions, the avoidance of disorder and the embracing and fostering of confusion, is the best position: *It is wise to keep in touch with chaos.*

This would enable us to offer literature to children in the most meaningful fashion. For if I have any dreams, any idyll of the world of children's literature, it would be that we cease to think of the "right" books for all children and offer to each individual child the "right" book for that child. The rank commercialism of book clubs that offer "the books your child needs to get into college"—any book club, in fact, that operates on the premise that no child can grow up properly or learn to read properly without a given set of books—is a downright fraud. It is somewhat similar to the field of poetry, wherein a well-known educator supposes that one perfect poem will entice all children into loving and understanding poetry. In the current jargon, "there just ain't no such animal." And I deplore methodology that tries to sell us on this very bitter pill.

It is my feeling that because each of us is an individual with particular sensitivities, background, outlook and experience in life and dream of tomorrow, each of us alone can determine in what book, what piece of literature, those qualities live that will be meaningful to children, help them to grow, lead them on. The main point is to keep an open mind. Emerson called it self-reliance. It does not depend on some so-called book reviewer, some listing in a special catalog, the opinion of an expert.

Twenty years ago I was perfectly willing and able to adhere to and recommend a given list of books *sine qua non*; today I find myself in a position where I strongly feel that a pragmatic approach is oftentimes better. Disorder, confusion, chaos are strange bedfellows.

Yet there are many touchstones. First, that we do not avoid chaos, pretending that it doesn't exist. Second, that we attempt to meet it through literature (not just the kind of books that are poor substitutes), and third, that we find somewhere within ourselves that dream of what might be that will serve as a guide to our evaluation. It is a corollary, of course, that we keep uppermost in our mind the child's dream. It also follows that the dream must be true; it must have some meaning in terms of the child's growth and future, and the future of all mankind.

We take in hand the "quick of another human being" when we introduce a child to a book. And any librarian or teacher or parent who does not understand this robs children of what George Steiner calls the right to "private discovery" and "passionate digression," two of the most precious possessions of any human being and certainly two areas of growth, of dreaming, not to be found on the movie or television screen.

How often has the "private discovery" of a child, reading a story, a poem, been squelched by questions for a book report, an examination, a story read with interruptions to run to the dictionary and look up a word? What is the *right* answer and who is the voice *ex cathedra* who can interpret a piece of literature for everyone? Who has the right to interfere with "passionate digression," that wandering off from the main theme or plot or characters to savor a passage, an idea, a few spellbinding words that we remember all of our lives, long after the author or date or title of the book may have been forgotten?

These acts can never be the same for any two people, and they are happenings that occur irrespective of the immediate response that may happen to cross the face of the reader. Everyone has discovered that in reading to children it is impossible to tell immediately what moment, what words, what insights have flashed across the mind or touched the emotions. In my own experience I remember not only children but adults who seemed not to be listening to the poems I read, yet would write to me months later or come up to me years later with the query, "What was the poem you read about pigs?" or "Where can I find a copy of 'Macavity, the Mystery Cat'?"

This is why testing, as practiced in most schools, fails in the field of literature; indeed, it even loses thousands of children to literature, for it neglects to ask the essential questions: How does this book, this conversation, this passage, help a particular child to look at life? What identification does the individual make with a character or situation? What special moments or words or visions plant themselves deep into the mind and heart of a boy or girl? There are no immediate answers to these questions.

We have been for too long busy training the mind at the expense of the emotions. We have been concentrating so long on the comprehension—that is, the complete understanding of something—that we pass by the most important of early experiences, that of apprehension, the first grasping of the spirit of what is being given to us as individuals in our own lives. "Nothing can be perceived by the mind," wrote John Locke, "unless it has been first perceived by the senses."

We must continually remember what it was to have the heart of a child. There are those who would have us believe that such advances have been made in technology and learning that somehow the child's heart has changed in the process. I question this. I know that today's children are far more armed with facts, far more questioning than those who were children a decade or two ago. But does this change at all the essential hopes, fears, and dreams of inexperienced human beings? In a confused world would not these dreams be intensified and the searching for identification with the world become even stronger, more important?

Archibald MacLeish told us in the 1950s that the "crime of our civilization is that we do not feel." This message is outdated today. People everywhere are feeling keenly about their individuality, their dissatisfactions, their goals. Does it not follow that our children must be searching equally hard?

It is wise to keep in touch with chaos. It is wise to remember that when we teach literature, we are indeed taking an emotional risk. It is also wise to understand that we have in ourselves, in the books we share, the power to make chaos, confusion, and disorder positive and creative weapons, for they can become, within the heart and the imagination of a single child, an answer to dreams—and even perhaps our own.

Climb Into the
Bell Tower

The boy with a wolf's foot
runs through the streets howling
crying help me, do something
about this pain at the base of my spine
which has crept down into my toes
how can I kick a football
ride a bicycle
with a condition like mine
oh help me, but the people
shut their windows
stuff red cottonwool up their chimneys
black treacle in the keyholes
and train their eyes on electric rabbits
not to see him
they set up two government commissions to study him
one at the north pole
one at the south
two government commissions are studying his problems
and will report in five years' time.
The boy with a wolf's foot
risking hydrophobia

weeps tears of brine
which flow under their gates and
water their crocuses
oh those salty crocuses will be
bitter as lime
the boy with a wolf's foot
carries his schoolbag to the desert
after a picnic of tears and cod's roe, plants his flag
and waits for a sign
meanwhile the old black-coated bellringers
head down like ants on business
backwards like diesel engines
doggedly mumbling, climb
into the bell tower
lost in a cloud of charcoal
they ring their tocsin
but a venomous wind
carries the notes westward
and the boy with a wolf's foot
will not hear their chime.

We have all seen this boy of whom Joan Aiken writes in
The Skin Spinners, with his schoolbag and salty tears, entering the library—sometimes alone, often whisked in with a
group of others. He'll need a book, a thin book, because
he is desperate over an assignment. He'll check it out, bring
it back when he remembers, smudged with water stains
or greasy cod roe. *Help me—help me—oh help me.*

There is one way to help him, leaving the work in the
back room that needed finishing yesterday, to find out where
there is information on bicycles, on salt or diesels and
electric rabbits, showing him how to use the Dewey decimal
system and card catalog and where the encyclopedia is

shelved. But what happens on the day he appears again with one of his sneakers off, and in place of a sock are four furry toes? There is panic in his eyes:

> . . . help me, do something
> about this pain at the base of my spine
> which has crept down into my toes

A boy with a wolf's foot? A medical encyclopedia? Something in science fiction? The school nurse is not in until next week, the doctor listed on his chart in the main office is out on an emergency. His teacher is overseeing recess in the yard. His parents work. Surely there are people who will know what to do—

> . . . but the people
> shut their windows
> stuff red cottonwool up their chimneys
> black treacle in the keyholes
> and train their eyes on electric rabbits
> not to see him

The city health services, the state board of health? Their computers are broken down, but they will report it and

> . . . set up two government commissions to study him
> one at the north pole
> one at the south
> two government commissions are studying his problems
> and will report in five years' time

Five years is too late. Oh help me, he cries, his tears falling into the plants, over the desk, onto the floor, and over his foot. Wait here, he is told. The alarm is sounded and

. . . the old black-coated bellringers
head down like ants on business
backwards like diesel engines
doggedly mumbling, climb
into the bell tower
lost in a cloud of charcoal
they ring their tocsin

But even as this happens the boy has disappeared, leaving in the streets and the crocus beds great pools of tears; he has gone off into the desert, waiting for a sign. And the wind that whips up engulfs the sound of the alarm. The boy is lost . . . *help me, oh help me*, and the air grows dark.

There is no poem that can live, come alive, without a reader. The reader, the listener, breathes into each work of art his own experience, his own sensitivity, and re-creates it in meaningful terms. There is not, I think, one of us here who cannot identify with a boy's cry for help, and probably not a one of us who is unfamiliar with his frustrations. On a simple informational level we can all locate the cause and cure of hydrophobia.

But what we will do when we see him, howling for help, terrorized over the transformation, the wolf's foot, is another matter. Joan Aiken has not put us into her poem, for it would be quite another legend if she had. And so it is with great presumption that I venture a few guesses, because I think I know that school librarians have shown themselves to be not only highly capable but most imaginative in their responses to the outrageous situation.

I did not know you when I was growing up in Nebraska. I had never heard the term "school librarian," but I do remember in fourth grade a small, narrow shelf tacked to the wall that was called "the library." There were never more than half a dozen books there, such as any class member cared to bring from home and share. My contribution was a copy of Hans Christian Andersen's *The Snow Queen*, a large, thinnish book with a picture on the cover of Gerta and Kay adrift on an icy pond. It would be tempting for me to have reread this story long before now, but I won't, for it remains, along with *Alice's Adventures in Wonderland*, one of the few keys I have, most personally, to books as I remember them—not what they *are* to the adult in me, but what they *were* to the child in me that lives. I speak now of the important difference between comprehension, the complete understanding, and apprehension, the almost unconscious awareness of what is rumbling beneath the words, the intuitive understanding, if you will. *The Snow Queen*, then, as now, was about the friendship of a boy and a girl for each other, interrupted by something evil. A glass sliver in Kay's eye, a painful separation, but something to make everything all right again in the end. It is undoubtedly a flaw in my character, but I tend to view literature and art in terms of apprehension, and I suspect children do too. I am speaking of literature now, and not just books. Literature, in my terms, deals in symbols broad enough to reach beyond the specific, to engage the reader in a dialogue not only with universals but with himself, as part of that universe. So, if the sliver in Kay's eye appeared to me as an apprehension of evil, I was able then, and now, to put a hundred names to that evil in other forms.

There was no school librarian in my life at any time until my college years. Perhaps that is why I somewhat envy the children who have *you*—because I have seen in my adult life, both professionally, as a teacher, and as a parent, the impact that can be made on young people, the answers you have found to *help me.*

We are going to change the legend now. Looking at ourselves through this poem individually and collectively is not only possible, it is urgent. The times are not the best, and though we deplore the fact, a boy *is* running howling through the streets, oftentimes in the very streets where his own people do not know how to help him. Or if he runs in streets far from home, he will certainly not be surprised to find not only cottonwool stuffed up the chimneys but cottonwool dyed with the color of rage and anger.

We, as readers of this poem, can imagine for ourselves what sort of people inhabit these houses. As librarians you are keenly aware of the implications, for some of them you know as they grumble about the taxes they must pay to maintain your salaries, watch over your shoulder, and often challenge the books you have selected. Even while you are celebrating the International Year of the Child, they label it a "Communist farce." Even as you check out copies of *The Scarlet Letter*, *Brave New World*, *Pinocchio*, Judy Blume, and Maurice Sendak, they are burning these books along with hundreds of other titles and authors. They are busy writing their own books, introducing bills into state legislatures to pressure you into buying books that depict "the traditional roles of men and women, boys and girls" and books that show "absolute values of right and wrong."

The boy in the street does not concern them. It is wrong for him to be howling, displaying pain. He is not a proper symbol of community values, this boy whom they were done with when they paid their taxes so that you, and the teachers in your schools, would teach him "*how* to read." Their duty was done. Their windows are shut. Their doors are filled with treacle, an old antidote against disease.

"Men who burn books," George Steiner has written, "know what they are doing." And yet, do they always know what they are doing? If we do want to help, might we not find somewhere in the American Association of School Librarians Policies and Procedures for Selection of Instructional Materials a clue as to how we might climb up and pull the cottonwool a bit loose, dissolve the treacle, and offer information to these people who seemingly want no part of it? Is there a chink left open in the windows? Their minds and hearts? Because we abide by the tenet that we should "place principle above personal opinion and reason above prejudice"—can there be some way to present this to the people as well as to children? To open our libraries to the community so that its members can see that our selection provides the sort of information that represents their interest as well as that of "the others" of whom they disapprove, to invite them to read the books on the shelves and hold open forums in which values may be discussed and opinions aired? To try to lead perhaps only *one* individual into some new patterns of thinking? To encourage them to abide by their own beliefs, rather than those of list makers from other communities (and I refer here to the Island Trees incident)? To suggest that literature can answer, broaden, and change—if you will—an image that they may have been, through hearsay, given falsely?

It seems to me that the time is here when we must make the greatest effort of our careers to call upon our imaginations, to dream the wildest of dreams as to what potential you, as school librarians, have. Librarians/media specialists are no longer the men and women who give lessons on the Dewey decimal system and how to be quiet, share picture books, allow classes "library time," and fulfill basic requirements. Librarians are highly important members of a community, a city, a state, and a country threatened by the specter of those who would make us think alike, who are afraid of the antithesis of any idea they hold sacred—afraid, in short, to let the individual choose. We are allowing those who do not want us to think divergent thoughts to control our thoughts, to corner us, and possibly to destroy us.

Are we the parents and grandparents who will be led kicking and screaming to the chocolate factory where *they* want us to live? Or will we have to learn to fight with all the power we have to maintain the homes where we prefer to stay? The question is rhetorical.

As for the government and its studies, I do not think there is a person here who cannot make an impact, even in the act of casting a ballot. I grant you that it grows more and more difficult as the current trends toward reversing Supreme Court decisions mount, as elements in our society strive to turn time back. A most incessant gnawing arouses my own curiosity these days, as I begin to inquire into the history studies of my college years, throwing aside apprehension to arrive at comprehension. Are we reliving the days of the Puritans, some born the elect and some the damned? On what dates will the witch trials start? I have put on my summer reading list the essays of Emerson:

> What is man born for, but to be a Reformer, a Reformer of what man has made; a renouncer of lies; a restorer of truth and good. . . .

and Thoreau's "Essay on the Duty of Civil Disobedience."

If the crocus is drowned in salt, it will not come up again in the spring. It will die in its own bitterness. Perhaps we had better go armed with spades and plant new gardens—yes, even for those who seal their windows against us.

"The purposes of school education," John Dewey wrote, "is to insure the continuance of education by organizing the powers that insure growth." We, who are in school every day, know that it is through these powers that children will grow, and that we ourselves must never stop growing. And every book we put on our shelves is part of this insurance.

We do have unmatched power: the power of the book. We are the power holders, for we select and we distribute this power each time we offer a book. There is nothing else like the book for what George Steiner describes as "private discovery" and "passionate digression." No film or filmstrip, no element of the media allows for the ideas and dreams that live within the book, passages to which the individual can turn again and again for new thoughts, new insights, new images, new solutions to individual and collective problems.

It is in our power to rise above mediocrity. I had an opportunity, as one of nine judges for the five winners in the children's field for the American Book Awards, to reject the mediocre books that in my opinion were harmful.

I think, with some humor, about a picture book with a lengthy foreword telling me that "this beautiful children's book is a remarkable achievement . . . that will be passed down for generations," how the child will "look at the

pictures over mother or daddy's shoulder, or sit on grandmother or grandfather's lap while being read to," how children will eagerly read it, "how vividly a mouse being sent
to a city of cats, to bring a message from God, portrays
the fear Jonah felt when he sailed off in a completely opposite
direction from the one God had commanded him." I do
not make light of the story of Jonah or of the Bible, but
full-color illustrations of cats dressed in sackcloth, or Jonah
as a mouse commanding a cowering cat-queen, are too
much!

I cannot dismiss quite so easily a work of fiction in which
camp counselors allow a boy in his early teens to assume
responsibility and make decisions for a mentally disturbed
younger camper, nor a book where a mother is completely
insensitive to the privacy and physical/emotional needs of
a growing boy, nor yet another novel where on the first
page the same phrase is repeated three times (and all of
the last three by well-known, popular authors). It is probably
another flaw in my character that I remain disturbed by a
recent tendency in any number of "best book lists" to choose
the surreal, the disturbing, the grotesque, and the bizarre.
I am constantly reminded by those to whom I say this that
children do enjoy being frightened, that they do understand
the difference between the real and the fantasy world, and
yet I wonder. The devil in *Faust*, the wild things, the witch
in *Hansel and Gretel*, the giant in *Jack and the Beanstalk*
are important as symbols of those things that must be con-
trolled. Yet there are many books nowadays that foster a
fright and insecurity all too prevalent in our world. In folk-
tales and fairy tales, in true fantasy, there is always some
help, some magic word, some wise adult. And although

there is the magic word of *Jumanji* in the Caldecott winner, I wonder about the value of the adult's laughter *interrupting* Peter's attempt to recount what had happened while the parents were away.

Far worse, to my mind, than frank sexual explanations or even, when used in the correct context, explicits, is the cop-out of writer or editor, seeking sales in the guise of "relevancy," relinquishing all responsibility to point out that there is help and hope for the reader. It may be an understanding adult, it may only be a magic word, it may be simply an idea that needs "private discovery," but it is there for the reader to seize.

There is hope, and there is imagination in conceiving of ways to reach people, government, replanting crocuses so they will bloom again. But we must remember, above all, the help and hope of the child. If no one else listens to the howling of the boy, it falls to us. Ours is the power to change his life. We have all we need to give him that help and hope. We have the time, the money, the power, and the imagination.

But lest someone should tell us there is no time, we must tell them that no one has time; time must be *made*, yes, even time from our personal lives. It is not easy to make, but it can be done. But what *is* easy that is, in the end, worthwhile?

And lest someone bemoan slashed funds and lack of money, I would tell you a story I heard about a school in the Los Angeles area without a library and books and a pittance of a budget. Time and imagination sent the children of the school out into the community on a spelling bee. For ten cents the children would spell words for the people in the neighborhoods, all proceeds to go toward the purchase of books. In a short time over two thousand dollars was raised, the children were applying themselves to learning, and the community was far happier that not only its tax money was being spent well in the schools but that their pin money was also helping to educate both old and young. Another way, perhaps, to get to the people?

We have the power; even though some of us should choose not to pull out cottonwool or dissolve treacle or go to the polls, yet we can still operate. We can refuse to buy mediocre books that offer no hope, no help, and have no symbolic worth. We can pass up books with alluring dust jackets that camouflage a paucity of inner content. We can balk at the bizarre, the unresolved ego wish of a writer or artist who speaks not for children but for himself alone; we can cast a jaundiced eye on lists or studies that purport to contain the books *every* child should read; we can, if we must, be our own book reviewers, not relying on anyone else to know what is good for us or the children we serve. We can trust our intuition. We can summon our imagination, an asset most children and many adults lack today, by displaying imagination in ourselves, that elusive and rare quality by which worlds can be changed.

And when the boy with a wolf's foot comes to us crying "oh help me," *we* can ease his pain. We can find on our library shelves dozens, hundreds, thousands of books that tell the story of those who have learned to live with the foot of a wolf—blindness, broken homes, poverty, ignorance, bigotry, persecution, and illness. We will take the boy's hand so that he does *not* run off to the desert. We will brave the venomous winds, spawned by book burnings and the hot air of rabble-rousers. We will, in short, depose the doggedly mumbling black-coated bellringers and go (backwards like diesel engines if necessary, but *go*) up the stairway. We will attack the cloud of charcoal and destroy it. Even in the face of venomous winds, we will sound the alarm and sound it again.

We are the bellringers. It is we who must climb into the bell tower.

And the boy with a wolf's foot will have his sign.

Sources

"The Poem on Page 81" was written in rebuttal to an article by Patrick Groff and published in *Top of the News*, November 1967, vol. 24, no. 1.

"Beginnings" was given at the National Council of Teachers of English convention in Chicago in 1976 and subsequently published in *Language Arts*, March 1978, vol. 55, no. 3.

"Edward Lear: A Legacy of Hope" was published in *Writers for Children* (New York: Charles Scribner's Sons, 1987).

"David McCord: The Singer, the Song, and the Sung" was published in *The Horn Book*, February 1979, vol. 55, no. 1.

"Nine Poets of the Child's World: Behn, Ciardi, Farber, Jarrell, Kennedy, Merriam, Prelutsky, Silverstein, Worth." Behn, Ciardi, Jarrell: published in *Twentieth Century Children's Writers*, 1st edition (New York: St. Martin's Press, 1978). Farber, Merriam, Prelutsky: published in the 2nd edition, 1983. Kennedy, Worth: published in the 3rd edition, 1989. Silverstein: published in abridged form in *The New York Times Book Review*, 1986.

"Mendacious Dwarfs and Mountebanks" was given for *The Horn Book* 60th Anniversary Celebration at the American Library Association convention in Dallas, Texas, in 1984.

"Imagination: The Forms of Things Unknown" was given at the Language Arts conference of the National Council of Teachers of English regional meeting in Portland, Oregon, in 1981 and subsequently published in *The Horn Book*, June 1982, vol. 58, no. 3.

"The Voice of the Poet" was given at the University of Georgia in 1983 and published in *The Advocate*, Fall 1983, vol. 3, no. 1.

"Literature, Creativity, and Imagination" was given at a joint symposium of the Children's Book Council and the Association for Child Education in Los Angeles in 1971. It was subsequently published in *Childhood Education*, April 1972, vol 48, no. 7, and in 1973 as a pamphlet with articles on the same subject by Lloyd Alexander and Virginia Hamilton and a preface by Beman Lord, and has since been reprinted.

"Children's Literature—A Creative Weapon" was given at the University of Toledo, Ohio, in June 1972 as "Children's Literature–In Chaos, A Creative Weapon." First published in *The Reading Teacher*, March 1974, vol. 27, no. 6, and reprinted in *Using Literature and Poetry Affectively*, edited by Jon Shapiro, International Reading Association, 1980.

"Climb Into the Bell Tower" was given at the awards luncheon at the annual American Library Association conference in Philadelphia, Pennsylvania, in 1982. It was subsequently published in *School Library Media Quarterly*, Winter 1983, vol. 11, no. 2.

Acknowledgments

Every effort has been made to trace the ownership of all copyrighted material and to secure the necessary permission to reprint these selections. In the event of any question arising as to the use of any material, this editor and the publisher, while expressing regret for any inadvertent error, will be happy to make the necessary correction in future printings. Thanks are due to the following for permission to reprint the copyrighted materials listed below:

Joan Aiken for "The Boy With a Wolf's Foot" from *The Skin Spinners*, copyright © 1976 by Joan Aiken. Used by permission of the author.

Curtis Brown, Ltd. for "My Dragon" by X. J. Kennedy, from *The Phantom Ice Cream Man*, published by Atheneum (Macmillan). Copyright © 1975, 1977, 1978, 1979 by X. J. Kennedy. Reprinted by permission of Curtis Brown, Ltd.

Doubleday for "Have You Watched the Fairies?" by Rose Fyleman, from *Fairies and Chimneys* by Rose Fyleman, copyright 1918, 1929 by George H. Doran. "Dinky" and "Praise to the End!" from *The Collected Poems of Theodore Roethke* by Theodore Roethke. "Dinky" copyright 1953 by Theodore Roethke; "Praise to the End!" copyright 1950 by Theodore Roethke. All poems used by permission of Doubleday, a division of Bantam, Doubleday, Dell Publishing Group, Inc.

E. P. Dutton, for the excerpt from *Borges on Writing*, edited by Norman Thomas di Giovanni, Daniel Halpern, and Frank MacShane. Copyright © 1972, 1973 by Jorge Luis Borges, Norman Thomas di Giovanni, Daniel Halpern, and Frank MacShane. Reprinted by permission of the publisher, E. P. Dutton, a division of Penguin Books USA Inc.

Farrar, Straus & Giroux, Inc. for "Clock," "Frog," "Grass," "Marbles," and "Porches" from *Small Poems* by Valerie Worth, copyright © 1972 by Valerie Worth. "Asparagus," "Beetle," "Coat Hangers," and "Telephone Poles," from *Small Poems Again* by Valerie Worth, copyright © 1975, 1986 by Valerie Worth. "Earthworms," "Fireworks," "Hose," "Lawnmower," "Lions," "Magnet," "Mosquito," "Safety Pin," "Sea Lions," "Shoes," and "Sparrow," from *More Small Poems* by Valerie Worth, copyright © 1976 by Valerie Worth. "Garbage," "Mushroom," and "Slug," from *Still More Small Poems* by Valerie Worth, copyright © 1976, 1977, 1978 by Valerie Worth. Reprinted by permission of Farrar, Straus and Giroux, Inc.

Robert Froman for "Greedy" from *Street Poems* by Robert Froman. Copyright © 1971 by Robert Froman. Reprinted by permission of the author.

Greenwillow Books for "The Ghoul" from *Nightmares* by Jack Prelutsky. Copyright © 1976 by Jack Prelutsky. Last stanza from "The Zombie" from *The Headless Horseman Rides Tonight* by Jack Prelutsky. Copyright © 1980 by Jack Prelutsky. Reprinted by permission of Greenwillow Books (A Division of William Morrow and Company, Inc.).

Harcourt Brace Jovanovich, Inc. for "Digging for China" from *Things of This World* by Richard Wilbur, copyright © 1956 and renewed 1984 by Richard Wilbur, reprinted by permission of Harcourt Brace Jovanovich, Inc.

Harper & Row, Publishers, Inc. for "About the Teeth of Sharks" from *You Read to Me, I'll Read to You* by John Ciardi (J. B. Lippincott). Copyright © 1962 by John Ciardi. "Ations" and last two lines from "The Toad and the Kangaroo" from *A Light in the Attic* by Shel Silverstein. Copyright © 1981 by Evil Eye Music, Inc. "Sarah Cynthia Sylvia Stout Would Not Take the Garbage Out" from *Where the Sidewalk Ends* by Shel Silverstein. Copyright © 1974 by Evil Eye Music, Inc. All reprinted by permission of Harper & Row, Publishers, Inc.

David Higham Associates Ltd. for excerpt from "Fern Hill" from *The Poems of Dylan Thomas*. Copyright 1945 by the Trustees for the Copyrights of Dylan Thomas. Reprinted by permission of David Higham Associates Ltd.

Felice Holman for "The City Dump" from *At the Top of my Voice and Other Poems* by Felice Holman. Copyright © 1970 by Felice Holman. Reprinted by permission of the author.

Henry Holt and Company, Inc. for "The Pasture," and "Stopping By Woods on a Snowy Evening" by Robert Frost. Copyright © 1923, 1930 by Holt, Rinehart and Winston and renewed 1951, 1958 by Robert Frost. Reprinted from *The Poetry of Robert Frost* edited by Edward Connery Lathem, by permission of Henry Holt and Company, Inc.

The Horn Book, Inc. for excerpt from "Where Are We Going with Poetry for Children?" article by Patrick J. Groff in *The Horn Book Magazine*, August 1966, pp. 456–463. Reprinted by permission of The Horn Book, Inc.

Houghton Mifflin Company for excerpts from: *The Hobbit* by J.R.R. Tolkien, copyright © 1966 by J.R.R. Tolkien; and *Adventures of Tom Bombadil* by J.R.R. Tolkien, copyright © 1962 by George Allen & Unwin, Ltd. Both reprinted by permission of Houghton Mifflin Company.

Instructor Books for "Words" by Veronica Keillor from *The Poetry Place Anthology* copyright © 1983. Reprinted by permission of Instructor Books.

X. J. Kennedy for excerpts from: "At the laundromat Liz Meyer" from *Brats*. Copyright © 1986. Published by Margaret K. McElderry Books/Atheneum; "Tyrannosaur" from *Did Adam Name the Vinegarroon?*", copyright © 1982, published by David R. Godine; "Bat," "Maturity," "Mole," "Rain into River," "Roofscape," and "To a Forgetful Wishing Well" from *The Forgetful Wishing Well*, copyright © 1985, published by Margaret K. McElderry Books/Atheneum; "Cows," "Cocoa Skin Coat," "Exploding Gravy," "Giant Snail," "Instant Storm," "My Birthday Cake," "Snowflake Souffle," "Waking Up Uncle," and "The Whales Off Wales" from *One Winter Night in August and Other Nonsense Rhymes*, copyright © 1975, published by Margaret K. McElderry/Atheneum; "All four of my Uncle Erics," "Television Charmer," "My Mother's Mad for Bargain Sales," "Cousin Carrée's Cubic Cuisine," "A Ticklish Recipe," and section headings: Cheerful Spirits, Far-Out Family, Unheard-Of Birds and Couldn't Be Beasts from *The Phantom Ice Cream Man: More Nonsense Verse*, copyright © 1979, published by Margaret K. McElderry Books/Atheneum. All reprinted by permission of the author.

Little, Brown and Company for excerpts from "Glowworm," "No Present Like the Time," "The Adventure of Chris," "Far Away," "August 28," "The Walnut Tree," "Queer," "Up the Pointed Ladder," "Song," "Star in the Pail," "Marty's Party," "Bananas and Cream," "In Winter Sky," "Books Fall Open," "Watching the Moon," "Ants and Sailboats," "Five Chants (Part 3)," "Take Sky," "Alphabet (Eta Z)," "That's Not," "Alley Cat," and "Blessed Lord" from *One At a Time* by David McCord. Copyright © 1952, renewed © 1961, 1962, 1965, 1966, 1970, 1974 by David McCord. "Go Fly a Saucer" from *The Old Bateau and Other Poems* by David McCord. Copyright 1953 by David McCord. Reprinted by permission of Little, Brown and Company. And for "This was a Poet" from *The Complete Poems of Emily Dickinson*, edited by Thomas H. Johnson. Copyright © 1929 by Martha Dickinson Bianchi; © renewed 1957 by Mary L. Hampson. By permission of Little, Brown and Company. Reprinted by permission of the publishers and the Trustees of Amherst College from *The Poems of Emily Dickinson*, edited by Thomas H. Johnson, Cambridge, Mass. The Belknap Press of Harvard University Press, Copyright 1951, © 1955, 1979, 1983 by the President and Fellows of Harvard College.

Liveright Publishing Corporation for "hist whist" from *Tulips & Chimneys* by E. E. Cummings. "hist whist" is reprinted from TULIPS & CHIMNEYS by E. E. Cummings, Edited by George James Firmage, by permission of Liveright Publishing Corporation. Copyright 1923, 1925 and renewed 1951, 1953 by E. E. Cummings. Copyright © 1973, 1976 by the Trustees for the E. E. Cummings Trust. Copyright © 1973, 1976 by George James Firmage.

Macmillan Publishing Company for "Mr. 'Gator" from *Let's Marry Said the Cherry* by N. M. Bodecker. Copyright © 1974 by N. M. Bodecker. Reprinted with permission of Margaret K. McElderry Books, an imprint of Macmillan Publishing Company. "Varge," from *8 A.M. Shadows*, by Patricia Hubbell. Copyright © 1965 by Patricia Hubbell. Reprinted with permission of Atheneum Publishers, an imprint of Macmillan Publishing Company. Excerpts, including the full poem "The Bird of Night," from *The Bat-Poet* by Randall Jarrell. Copyright © Macmillan Publishing Company 1963, 1964. Reprinted with permission of Macmillan Publishing Company. Excerpt from "The Lost World, Part 1: Children's Arms" from *The Lost World* by Randall Jarrell. Copyright © Randall Jarrell 1963, 1965. Reprinted with permission of Macmillan Publishing Company. "The Little Turtle," from *Collected Poems* by Vachel Lindsay. Copyright 1920 by Macmillan Publishing Company, renewed 1948 by Elizabeth C. Lindsay. Reprinted with permission of Macmillan Publishing Company. "The Lion" and "An Explanation of the Grasshopper" from *Collected Poems* by Vachel Lindsay. (New York: Macmillan, 1925).

McKnight Gosewich Associates Agency Inc. for "Garbage Delight" by Dennis Lee, from *Garbage Delight* by Dennis Lee, copyright © 1977 by Dennis Lee and published by Macmillan of Canada. Reprinted with permission of McKnight Gosewich Associates Agency, Inc.

New Directions Publishing Corporation for excerpt from "Fern Hill" from *Poems of Dylan Thomas*. Copyright © 1945 by the Trustees for the Copyrights of Dylan Thomas. Reprinted by permission of New Directions Publishing Corporation.

The Putnam Publishing Group for three lines from "Like Me" by Dorothy Aldis. Reprinted by permission of G. P. Putnam's Sons from *All Together* by Dorothy Aldis, copyright 1925–1928, 1934, 1939, 1952, copyright renewed © 1953–1956, 1962, 1967 by Dorothy Aldis.

Random House, Inc. for "Me I Am!" by Jack Prelutsky from *The Random House Book of Poetry for Children*, selected and introduced by Jack Prelutsky. Copyright © 1983 by Random House, Inc. Reprinted by permission of the publisher.

Marian Reiner for "The Gnome" from *Windy Morning* by Harry Behn. Copyright 1953 by Harry Behn. Copyright © 1981 renewed by Alice Behn Goebel, Pamela Behn Adam, Prescott Behn and Peter Behn. "Seconds are bugs . . .", twenty-one line excerpt from *All Kinds of Time*, copyright 1950, published by Harcourt, Brace and Company. Excerpts from *Chrysalis, Concerning Children and Poetry*, copyright © 1968, published by Harcourt, Brace & World. "Curiosity" from *Windy Morning*, copyright © 1963, published by Harcourt, Brace and Company. All reprinted by permission of Marian Reiner. And for "Thumbprint" from *A Sky Full of Poems* by Eve Merriam. Copyright © 1964, 1970, 1973 by Eve Merriam. All Rights Reserved. Excerpts from: "Basic for Further Irresponsibility," "Neuteronomy," "Umbilical," and "The Wholly Family" from *Finding a Poem*, copyright © 1970, published by Atheneum; from *Independent Voices*, copyright © 1968, published by Atheneum; "A Cliché," "Having Words," "How to Eat a Poem," and " 'I' says the Poem" from *It Doesn't Always Have to Rhyme*, copyright © 1964, published by Atheneum; excerpt from *Rainbow Writing*, copyright © 1976, published by Atheneum; and "Supermarket, Supermarket" from *A Word or Two with You*, copyright © 1981, published by Atheneum. All reprinted by permission of Marian Reiner for the author.

Sidgwick & Jackson, Publishers for "After the Salvo" from *Poems, 1912–1933* by Herbert Asquith. Reprinted by permission of the publishers.

The Society of Authors for three lines from "Have You Watched the Fairies?" by Rose Fyleman. Reprinted by permission of The Society of Authors as the literary representative of the Estate of Rose Fyleman.

Swallow Press for excerpts from "What are the most unusual things you find in garbage cans?" by Jim Schevill. Reprinted by permission of Swallow Press/Ohio University Press.

Unwin Hyman Ltd. for extracts taken from *The Adventures of Tom Bombadil* by J.R.R. Tolkien, copyright © 1962 by George Allen & Unwin Ltd., and from *The Hobbit* by J.R.R. Tolkien, copyright © 1966 by J.R.R. Tolkien. Both reproduced by kind permission of Unwin Hyman Ltd.

A P Watt Ltd. for "The Forbidden Play" from *The Penny Fiddle* by Robert Graves. Reprinted by permission of A P Watt Limited on behalf of the Executors of the Estate of Robert Graves.

Wesleyan University Press for "The Mole" from *Winter News* by John Haines. Copyright © 1965 by John Haines. Reprinted by permission of Wesleyan University Press.

Bibliography

The Poem on Page 81

Asquith, Herbert. *Poems, 1912–1913*. London: Sidgwick & Jackson, Ltd., 1934.

Behn, Harry. *Windy Morning: Poems and Pictures*. New York: Harcourt, Brace & World, Inc., 1953.

Ciardi, John. *How Does a Poem Mean?* Boston: Houghton Mifflin Company, 1959.

Coleridge, Samuel. *Biographia Literaria*, Vols. I and II. J. Shawcross, ed. London: Oxford University Press, 1973.

Frost, Robert. *Complete Poems of Robert Frost*. New York: Holt, Rinehart and Winston, Inc., 1951.

Fyleman, Rose. *Fairies and Chimneys*. New York: George H. Doran Company, 1920.

Groff, Patrick. "Where Are We Going with Poetry for Children?" *The Horn Book*, August 1966.

Lindsay, Vachel. *The Congo and Other Poems*. New York: The Macmillan Company, 1924.

MacLeish, Archibald. *Poetry and Experience*. Boston: Houghton Mifflin Company, 1961.

McCord, David. *The Old Bateau and Other Poems*. Boston: Little, Brown and Company, 1953.

Moore, Marianne. *Collected Poems*. New York: The Macmillan Company, 1952.

Mumford, Lewis. *Green Memories: The Story of Geddes Mumford*. New York: Harcourt, Brace & World, Inc., 1947.

Sartre, Jean-Paul. *The Words*. New York: George Braziller, Inc., 1964.

Stephens, James. *The Crock of Gold*. New York: The Macmillan Company, 1960.

Stevens, Wallace. *Collected Poems*. New York: Alfred A. Knopf, Inc., 1954.

224

Taylor, Anne and Jane. *Rhymes for the Nursery.* London: Arthur Hall, Virtue & Co., 1860.

Tolkein, J.R.R. *The Fellowship of the Ring.* Boston: Houghton Mifflin Company, 1954.

———. *The Hobbit.* Boston: Houghton Mifflin Company, 1937.

Yevtushenko, Yevgeny. *A Precocious Autobiography.* New York: E. P. Dutton & Co., Inc., 1963.

Beginnings

Behn, Harry. *Cricket Songs.* New York: Harcourt, Brace & World, Inc., 1964.

Borges, Jorge Luis. *Borges on Writing,* Norman Thomas di Giovanni et al., eds. New York: E. P. Dutton & Co., Inc., 1973.

Huck, Charlotte. Quoted in "For the Members." *Language Arts,* January 1976.

Hunter, Mollie. *Talent Is Not Enough.* New York: Harper & Row, Publishers, 1976.

Larrick, Nancy. "Poets and Poetry in the 1975 Poetry Festival." *English Journal,* October 1975.

Lewis, Richard, ed. *Miracles: Poems of Children of the English-Speaking World.* New York: Simon and Schuster, 1966.

Livingston, Myra Cohn. "But Is It Poetry?" Part I, *The Horn Book,* December 1975. Part II, *The Horn Book,* February 1976.

———. *4-Way Stop and Other Poems.* New York: Atheneum Publishers, 1976.

———. *The Malibu and Other Poems.* New York: Atheneum Publishers, 1972.

———. *The Way Things Are and Other Poems.* New York: Atheneum Publishers, 1974.

———. *When You Are Alone/It Keeps You Capone: An Approach to Creative Writing with Children.* New York: Atheneum Publishers, 1973.

———. *Whispers and Other Poems.* New York: Harcourt, Brace and Company, 1958.

Montaigne, Michel de. "On Husbanding Your Will." Translated by Donald M. Frame. In *The Complete Works of Montaigne,* Essays III. Stanford, Calif.: Stanford University Press, 1957.

Rubel, William, and Mandel, Gerry. *The Editor's Notebook.* Santa Cruz, Calif.: Stone Soup, Incorporated, 1976.

Shakespeare, William. *The Tragedy of Hamlet, Prince of Denmark.*

Steiner, George. *Language and Silence.* New York: Atheneum Publishers, 1967.

Whitman, Ruth, and Feinberg, Harriet, eds. *Poemmaking: Poets in Classrooms.* Massachusetts Council of Teachers of English, 1975.

Edward Lear: A Legacy of Hope

Byrom, Thomas. *Nonsense and Wonder: The Poems and Cartoons of Edward Lear.* New York: E. P. Dutton & Co., Inc., 1977.

Chukovsky, Kornei. *From Two to Five*. Berkeley, Calif.: University of California Press, 1963.

Davidson, Angus. *Edward Lear: Landscape Painter and Nonsense Poet*. London: John Murray (Publishers) Ltd., 1938.

Hyman, Susan. *Edward Lear's Birds*. New York: William Morrow and Company, Inc., 1980.

Lear, Edward. *The Complete Nonsense Book*. New York: Dodd, Mead & Company, Inc., 1958.

————. *Edward Lear's Journals: A Selection*. Edited by Herbert van Thal. New York: Coward-McCann Inc., 1953.

————. *Later Letters of Edward Lear*. Lady Constance Strachey, ed. London: T. Fisher Unwin, 1911.

————. *Letters of Edward Lear*. Lady Constance Strachey, ed. London: T. Fisher Unwin, 1907.

Lehman, John. *Edward Lear and His World*. New York: Charles Scribner's Sons, 1977.

Noakes, Vivien. *Edward Lear: The Life of a Wanderer*. Boston: Houghton Mifflin Company, 1969; London: William Collins Sons & Co. Ltd., 1968.

Sewell, Elizabeth. *The Field of Nonsense*. London: Chatto & Windus, Ltd., 1952.

Silverstein, Shel. *A Light in the Attic: Poems and Drawings*. New York: Harper & Row Publishers, 1981.

Smith, William Jay. *Laughing Time*. New York: Delacorte Press, 1980.

————. " 'So They Smashed That Old Man . . .": A Note on Edward Lear." *The Horn Book*, August, 1959.

David McCord: The Singer, the Song, and the Sung

McCord, David. *One at a Time*. Boston: Little, Brown and Company, 1977.

————. *Pen, Paper, and Poem*. New York: Holt, Rinehart and Winston, Inc., 1973.

————. *Speak Up, More Rhymes of the Never Was and Always Is*. Boston: Little Brown and Company, 1980.

Nine Poets: Behn

Behn, Harry. *All Kinds of Time*. New York: Harcourt, Brace and Company, 1950.

————. *Chrysalis: Concerning Children and Poetry*. New York: Harcourt, Brace & World, Inc., 1968.

————. *Crickets and Bullfrogs and Whispers and Thunder: Poems and Pictures by Harry Behn*. Lee Bennett Hopkins, ed. New York; Harcourt Brace Jovanovich, Inc., 1984.

————. *The Faraway Lurs*. Cleveland: The World Publishing Company, 1963.

————. *The Golden Hive: Poems and Pictures*. New York: Harcourt, Brace & World, Inc., 1966.

————. *The House Beyond the Meadow*. New York: Pantheon Books, Inc., 1955.

————. *The Little Hill: Poems and Pictures by Harry Behn*. New York: Harcourt, Brace and Company, 1949.

————. *Omen of the Birds*. Cleveland: The World Publishing Company, 1954.

————. *The Painted Cave*. New York: Harcourt, Brace and Company, 1957.

————. *Roderick*. New York: Harcourt, Brace & World, Inc., 1957.

————. *The Two Uncles of Pablo*. New York: Harcourt, Brace and Company, 1959.

————. *What a Beautiful Noise*. Cleveland: The World Publishing Company, 1970.

————. *Windy Morning: Poems and Pictures by Harry Behn*. New York: Harcourt, Brace and Company, 1953.

————. *The Wizard in the Well: Poems and Pictures by Harry Behn*. New York: Harcourt, Brace and Company, 1956.

————, translator. *Cricket Songs: Japanese Haiku Translated by Harry Behn*. New York, Harcourt, Brace & World, Inc., 1964.

————. *More Cricket Songs: Japaniese Haiku Translated by Harry Behn*. New York: Harcourt Brace Jovanovich, Inc., 1971.

————, and Peter Beilenson. *Haiku Harvest: Japanese Haiku Series IV*. Mount Vernon, N.Y.: The Peter Pauper Press, 1962.

Nine Poets: Ciardi

Ciardi, John. *Dialogue with an Audience*. Philadelphia: J. B. Lippincott Co., 1963.

————. *Doodle Soup*. Boston: Houghton Mifflin Company, 1985.

————. *Fast and Slow: Poems for Advanced Children and Beginning Parents*. Boston: Houghton Mifflin Company, 1975.

————. *How does a Poem Mean?* Boston: Houghton Mifflin Company, 1960.

————. *I Met a Man*. Boston: Houghton Mifflin Company, 1961.

————. *John J. Plenty and the Fiddler Dan: A New Fable of the Grasshopper and the Ant*. Philadelphia: J. B. Lippincott Co., 1963.

————. *The Man Who Sang the Sillies*. Philadelphia: J. B. Lippincott Co., 1961.

————. *Manner of Speaking* (*Saturday Review* columns). New Brunswick, N.J.: Rutgers University Press, 1972.

————. *The Monster Den; or, Look What Happened at My House—and to It*. Philadelphia: J. B. Lippincott Co., 1959.

————. *The Reason for the Pelican*. Philadelphia: J. B. Lippincott Co., 1959.

————. *Someone Could Win a Polar Bear*. Philadelphia: J. B. Lippincott Co., 1970.

————. *You Know Who*. Philadelphia: J. B. Lippincott Co., 1963.

————. *You Read to Me, I'll Read to You*. Philadelphia: J. B. Lippincott Co., 1962.

Nine Poets: Farber

Farber, Norma. *As I Was Crossing Boston Common*. New York: E. P. Dutton & Co., Inc., 1975.

————. *How Does It Feel to be Old?* New York: E. P. Dutton & Co., Inc., 1979.

————. *How the Hibernators Came to Bethlehem.* New York: Walker Co., 1980.

————. *How the Left-Behind Beasts Built Ararat.* New York: Walker & Co., 1978.

————. *Never Say Ugh to a Bug.* New York: Greenwillow Books, 1979.

————. *Small Wonders.* New York: Coward, McCann & Geoghegan, 1979.

Nine Poets: Jarrell

Jarrell, Randall. *The Animal Family.* New York: Pantheon Books, Inc., 1965.

————. *The Bat-Poet.* New York: The Macmillan Company, 1964.

————. *Blood for a Stranger.* New York: Harcourt, Brace and Company, 1942.

————. *The Complete Poems.* New York: Farrar, Straus & Giroux, Inc., 1969.

————. *The Fisherman and His Wife.* New York: Farrar, Straus & Giroux, Inc., 1980.

————. *Fly by Night.* New York: Farrar, Straus & Giroux, Inc., 1976.

————. *The Gingerbread Rabbit.* New York: The Macmillan Company, 1964.

————. *Jerome: The Biography of a Poem.* New York: Grossman Publishers, 1971.

————. *Kipling, Auden, & Co.: Essays and Reviews 1935–1964.* New York: Farrar, Straus & Giroux, Inc., 1980.

————. *Little Friend, Little Friend.* New York: The Dial Press, Inc., 1945.

————. *The Lost World: New Poems.* New York: The Macmillan Company, 1965.

————. *Poetry and the Age.* New York: Alfred A. Knopf, Inc., 1953.

————. *A Sad Heart at the Supermarket: Essays and Fables.* New York: Atheneum Publishers, 1962.

————. *Selected Poems.* New York: Atheneum Publishers, 1964.

————. *Snow White and the Seven Dwarfs: A Tale from the Brothers Grimm.* New York: Farrar, Straus & Giroux, Inc., 1972.

————. *The Third Book of Criticism.* New York: Farrar, Straus & Giroux, Inc., 1969.

————. *The Woman at the Washington Zoo: Poems and Translations.* New York: Atheneum Publishers, 1960.

————, with Lore Segal. *The Juniper Tree and Other Tales from Grimm.* New York: Farrar, Straus & Giroux, Inc., 1973.

Nine Poets: Kennedy

Kennedy, X. J. *Brats.* New York: Margaret K. McElderry Books/Atheneum Publishers, 1986.

————. *Cross Ties: Selected Poems.* Athens, Ga.: University of Georgia Press, 1985.

————. *Did Adam Name the Vinegarroon?* Boston: David R. Godine, Publisher, Inc., 1982.

————. *Emily Dickinson in Southern California.* Boston: David R. Godine, Publishers, Inc., 1973.

———. *The Forgetful Wishing Well: Poems for Young People.* New York: Margaret K. McElderry Books/Atheneum Publishers, 1985.

———. *Ghastlies, Goops, & Pincushions: Nonsense Verse.* New York: Margaret K. McElderry Books/Atheneum Publishers, 1989.

———. *Growing into Love.* Garden City, N.Y.: Doubleday & Company, Inc., 1969.

———. *Hangover Mass.* Cleveland: Bits Press, 1984.

———, with Dorothy M. Kennedy. *Knock at a Star: A Child's Introduction to Poetry.* Boston: Little, Brown and Company, 1982.

———. *Nude Descending a Staircase.* Garden City, N.Y.: Doubleday & Company, Inc., 1961.

———. *One Winter Night in August and Other Nonsense Rhymes.* New York: Margaret K. McElderry Books/Atheneum Publishers, 1975.

———. *The Phantom Ice Cream Man: More Nonsense Verse.* New York: Margaret K. McElderry Books/Atheneum Publishers, 1979.

Nine Poets: Merriam

Merriam, Eve. *The Birthday Cow.* New York: Alfred A. Knopf, Inc., 1978.

———. *Blackberry Ink.* New York: William Morrow and Company, Inc., 1985.

———. *Catch a Little Rhyme.* New York: Atheneum Publishers, 1966.

———. *Chortles.* New York: William Morrow and Company, Inc., 1989.

———. *Finding a Poem.* New York: Atheneum Publishers, 1970.

———. *Fresh Paint.* New York: The Macmillan Company, 1986.

———. *Halloween ABC.* New York: The Macmillan Company, 1987.

———. *Independent Voices.* New York: Atheneum Publishers, 1968.

———. *The Inner City Mother Goose.* New York: Simon & Schuster, Inc., 1969.

———. *It Doesn't Always Have to Rhyme.* New York: Atheneum Publishers, 1964.

———. *Jamboree: Rhymes for All Times.* New York: Dell Publishing Co., Inc., 1984.

———. *Out Loud.* New York: Atheneum Publishers, 1973.

———. *Rainbow Writing.* New York: Atheneum Publishers, 1962.

———. *There Is No Rhyme for Silver.* New York: Atheneum Publishers, 1962.

———. *A Word or Two with You: New Rhymes for Young Readers.* New York: Atheneum Publishers, 1981.

———. *You Be Good and I'll Be Night.* New York: William Morrow and Company, Inc., 1988.

Nine Poets: Prelutsky

Prelutsky, Jack. *The Headless Horseman Rides Tonight: More Poems to Trouble Your Sleep.* New York: Greenwillow Books, 1980.

———. *The Mean Old Mean Hyena.* New York: Greenwillow Books, 1984.

———. *The New Kid on the Block.* New York: Greenwillow Books, 1984.

————. *Nightmares: Poems to Trouble Your Sleep.* New York: Greenwillow Books, 1978.

————. *The Queen of Eene.* New York: Greenwillow Books, 1978.

————. *Rolling Harvey down the Hill.* New York: Greenwillow Books, 1980.

————. *The Sheriff of Rottenshot.* New York: Greenwillow Books, 1982.

————. *The Snopp on the Sidewalk and Other Poems.* New York: Greenwillow Books, 1977.

————. *Tyrannosaurus Was a Beast.* New York: Greenwillow Books, 1988.

Nine Poets: Silverstein

Silverstein, Shel. *A Light in the Attic: Poems and Drawings.* New York: Harper & Row, Publishers, 1981.

————. *Where the Sidewalk Ends: The Poems and Drawings of Shel Silverstein.* New York: Harper & Row, Publishers, 1974.

Nine Poets: Worth

Worth, Valerie. *All the Small Poems.* New York: Farrar, Straus & Giroux,. Inc., 1987.

————. *More Small Poems.* New York: Farrar, Straus & Giroux, Inc., 1976.

————. *Small Poems.* New York: Farrar, Straus & Giroux, Inc., 1972.

————. *Small Poems Again.* New York: Farrar, Straus & Giroux, Inc., 1975.

————. *Still More Small Poems.* New York: Farrar, Straus & Giroux, Inc., 1978.

Mendacious Dwarfs and Mountebanks

Aldis, Dorothy. *All Together.* New York: G. P. Putnam's Sons, 1952.

Carroll, Lewis. *Alice's Adventures in Wonderland.* New York: Random House, Inc., 1946.

Dunning, Stephen ed. *Some Haystacks Don't Even Have Any Needle.* New York: Lothrop, Lee & Shepard Co., Inc., 1969.

Froman, Robert. *Street Poems.* New York: The McCall Publishing Company, 1971.

Graves, Robert. *The Penny Fiddle.* Garden City, N.Y.: Doubleday & Company, Inc., 1981.

Holman, Felice. *At the Top of My Voice and Other Poems.* New York: Charles Scribner's Sons, 1970.

Hubbell, Patricia. *8 A.M. Shadows.* New York: Atheneum Publishers, 1965.

Hughes, Ted. "Myth and Education." *Children's Literature in Education*, March 1970.

Lee, Dennis. *Garbage Delight.* Boston: Houghton Mifflin Company, 1977.

McCord, David. *One at a Time.* Boston: Little, Brown and Company, 1974.

Merriam, Eve. *It Doesn't Always Have to Rhyme.* New York: Atheneum Publishers, 1964.

Moore, Anne Carroll. *The Three Owls.* New York: The Macmillan Company, 1925.

Poetry Place Anthology. New York: Instructor Books, 1983.

Prelutsky, Jack, ed. *The Random House Book of Poetry for Children.* New York: Random House, Inc., 1983.

Silverstein, Shel. *Where the Sidewalk Ends: The Poems and Drawings of Shel Silverstein.* New York: Harper & Row, Publishers, 1974.

Steiner, George. "Short Shrift." *The New Yorker*, April 16, 1984.

Stephens, James. *The Crock of Gold.* New York, The Macmillan Company, 1964.

Watts, Isaac, D. D. *Horae Lyricae.* Vergennes, Vt.: Jepthah Shedd and Co., 1813.

Worth, Valerie. *Still More Small Poems.* New York: Farrar, Straus & Giroux, Inc., 1978.

Imagination: The Forms of Things Unknown

Blake, William. *Poetical Works of William Blake.* London: Oxford University Press, 1948.

Carroll, Lewis. *Through the Looking Glass and What Alice Found There.* New York: Random House, Inc., 1946.

Cole, William ed. *Poems of Magic and Spells.* New York: The World Publishing Company, 1960.

Cummings, E. E. *Complete Poems 1913–1962.* New York: Harcourt Brace Jovanovich, Inc., 1972.

Haines, John. *Winter News.* Middletown, Conn.: Wesleyan University Press, 1964.

Jarrell, Randall. *The Complete Poems.* New York: Farrar, Straus & Giroux, Inc., 1969.

Lindsay, Vachel. *Collected Poems.* New York: The Macmillan Company, 1973.

Roethke, Theodore. *Collected Poems of Theodore Roethke.* Garden City, N.Y.: Doubleday & Company, Inc., 1966.

Shakespeare, William. *A Midsummer Night's Dream.*

Tennyson, Alfred Lord. *The Poetic and Dramatic Works of Alfred, Lord Tennyson.* Boston: Houghton Mifflin Company, 1898.

Thomas, Dylan. *The Collected Poems of Dylan Thomas.* New York: New Directions Pub. Corp., 1957.

Wilbur, Richard. *Things of This World.* New York: Harcourt, Brace & World, Inc., 1956.

The Voice of the Poet

Aiken, Lucy, ed. *Poetry for Children.* London: Longman, Rees, Orme, Brown, and Green, 1831.

Bodeker, N. M. *Let's Marry Said the Cherry*. New York: Atheneum Publishers, 1974.

Carroll, Lewis. *Through the Looking Glass and What Alice Found There*. New York: Random House, Inc., 1946.

Chaucer, Geoffrey. *The Poetical Works of Chaucer*. F. N. Robinson, ed. Boston: Houghton Mifflin Company, 1933.

Ciardi, John. *You Read to Me, I'll Read to You*. New York: J. B. Lippincott, Co., 1962.

Cummings, E. E. *Complete Poems, 1913–1962*. New York: Harcourt Brace Jovanovich, Inc., 1972.

Decker, Marjorie. *The Christian Mother Goose Book*. Grand Junction, Colo.: Decker Press, Inc., 1978.

Decker, Marjorie. *The Christian Mother Goose Treasury*. Grand Junction, Colo.: C.M.G. Productions, Inc., 1980.

Dickinson, Emily. *The Complete Poems of Emily Dickinson*. Boston: Little, Brown and Company, 1960.

Gregory, Horace. *The Shield of Achilles*. New York: Harcourt, Brace and Company, 1944.

Herrick, Robert. *The Poetical Works of Robert Herrick*. London: Oxford University Press, 1921.

Kennedy, X. J. *The Phantom Ice Cream Man*. New York: Atheneum Publishers, 1978.

Merriam, Eve. *It Doesn't Always Have to Rhyme*. New York: Atheneum Publishers, 1964.

Merriam, Eve. *Finding a Poem*. New York: Atheneum Publishers, 1964.

Opie, Iona and Peter. *The Oxford Book of Children's Verse*. London: Oxford University Press, 1973.

———. *The Oxford Dictionary of Nursery Rhymes*. London: Oxford University Press, 1951.

Poetry Place Anthology. New York: Instructor Books, 1983.

Prelutsky, Jack. *The Headless Horseman Rides Tonight: More Poems to Trouble Your Sleep*. New York: Greenwillow Press, 1980.

———. *Nightmares: Poems to Trouble Your Sleep*. New York: Greenwillow Books, 1976.

Richards, I. A. *Science and Poetry*. London: Kegan Paul, Trench, Trubner & Co. Ltd., 1935.

Richards, Laura. *Tirra-Lirra*. Boston: Little, Brown and Company, 1955.

Sendak, Maurice. *Where the Wild Things Are*. New York: Harper & Row, Publishers, 1963.

Silverstein, Shel. *A Light in the Attic: Poems and Drawings*. New York: Harper & Row, Publishers, 1981.

———. *Where the Sidewalk Ends: The Poems and Drawings of Shel Silverstein*. New York: Harper & Row, Publishers, 1974.

Steiner, George. *Tolstoy or Dostoevsky: An Essay in the Old Criticism.* New York: Alfred A. Knopf, Inc., 1959.

Stevenson, Robert Louis. *A Child's Garden of Verses.* New York: Charles Scribner's Sons, 1895.

Taylor, Jane. *Original Poems.* New York: C. S. Francis & Co., 1854.

Tennyson, Alfred Lord. *The Poetic and Dramatic Works of Alfred, Lord Tennyson.* Boston: Houghton Mifflin Company, 1898.

Watts, Isaac, D. D. *Horae Lyricae.* Vergennes, Vt.: Jepthah Shedd and Co., 1813.

Literature, Creativity, and Imagination

Bishop, Elizabeth. *Ballad of the Burglar of Babylon.* New York: Farrar, Straus & Giroux, Inc., 1968.

Carroll, Lewis. *Through the Looking Glass and What Alice Found There.* New York: Random House, Inc., 1946.

Greenacre, Phyllis. *Swift and Carroll: A Psychoanalytic Study of Two Lives.* New York: International Universities Press, Inc., 1955.

Jarrell, Randall. *The Bat-Poet.* New York: The Macmillan Company, 1966.

Lewis, Richard, sel. *Miracles: Poems by Children of the English-Speaking World.* New York: Simon and Schuster, 1966.

MacLeish, Archibald. *Poetry and Experience.* Boston: Houghton Mifflin Company, 1961.

O'Neill, Mary. *Hailstones and Halibut Bones.* Garden City, N.Y.: Doubleday & Company, Inc., 1961.

Sendak, Maurice. *Higgledy Piggledy Pop!* or *There Must Be More to Life.* New York: Harper & Row, Publishers, 1967.

Spender, Stephen. "On Teaching Modern Poetry." In *Essays in Teaching*, Harold Taylor, ed. New York: Harper & Row, Publishers, 1950.

Steiner, George. *Language and Silence.* New York: Atheneum Publishers, 1965.

Children's Literature—A Creative Weapon

MacLeish, Archibald. *Poetry and Experience.* Boston: Houghton Mifflin Company, 1961.

Mumford, Lewis. *Green Memories: The Story of Geddes Mumford.* New York: Harcourt, Brace and Company, 1947.

Roethke, Theodore. *Straw for the Fire.* Garden City, N.Y.: Doubleday & Company, Inc., 1972.

Steiner, Garden. *Language and Silence.* New York: Atheneum Publishers, 1965.

Climb Into the Bell Tower

Aiken, Joan. *The Skin Spinners.* New York: The Viking Press, Inc., 1976.

Dewey, John. *Democracy and Education.* New York: The Free Press, 1916.

Emerson, Ralph Waldo. *Essays of Ralph Waldo Emerson.* Cambridge: Harvard University Press, 1987.

Mumford, Lewis. *Green Memories: The Story of Geddes Mumford.* New York: Harcourt, Brace & World, Inc., 1947.

"Policies and Procedures for Selection of Instructional Materials." *American Assoc. of School Librarians Notes*, Winter, 1977.

Steiner, George. *Language and Silence.* New York: Atheneum, 1967.

"Textbook Content Standards Act" of The American Legislative Exchange Council (ALEC), in *People for the American Way Bulletin*, May, 1982.

"The Island Trees Case Turns Another Legal Corner." (Story on Island Trees school district of Long Island, quoting Frank Martin of the Island Tree Board of Education.) *The New York Times*, June 27, 1982.

Wood, Rev. David A. *Reminder News*, April 22, 1981.

Index